HOW THEY
BLEW IT

HOW THEY BLEW IT

The CEOs and entrepreneurs behind some of the world's most catastrophic business failures

Jamie Oliver & Tony Goodwin

KoganPage

LONDON PHILADELPHIA NEW DELHI

The authors acknowledge that they have drawn on a great many sources to write this narrative, and as it would interrupt the narrative to acknowledge every instance, a list of sources is given at the end of each chapter.

Publisher's note
Every possible effort has been made to ensure that the information contained in this book is accurate at the time of going to press, and the publishers and authors cannot accept responsibility for any errors or omissions, however caused. No responsibility for loss or damage occasioned to any person acting, or refraining from action, as a result of the material in this publication can be accepted by the editor, the publisher or any of the authors.

First published in Great Britain and the United States in 2010 by Kogan Page Limited

120 Pentonville Road	525 South 4th Street, #241	4737/23 Ansari Road
London N1 9JN	Philadelphia PA 19147	Daryaganj
United Kingdom	USA	New Delhi 110002
www.koganpage.com		India

© Jamie Oliver and Tony Goodwin, 2010

The right of Jamie Oliver and Tony Goodwin to be identified as the authors of this work has been asserted by them in accordance with the Copyright, Designs and Patents Act 1988.

| ISBN | 978 0 7494 6065 5 |
| E-ISBN | 978 0 7494 5965 9 |

British Library Cataloguing-in-Publication Data

A CIP record for this book is available from the British Library.

Library of Congress Cataloging-in-Publication Data

Oliver, Jamie, 1973–
  How they blew it : the CEOs and entrepreneurs behind some of the world's most catastrophic business failures / Jamie Oliver, Tony Goodwin. -- 1st ed.
    p. cm.
  Includes index.
  ISBN 978-0-7494-6065-5 -- ISBN 978-0-7494-5965-9 1. Chief executive officers. 2. Businesspeople. 3. Executive ability. 4. Success in business--Moral and ethical aspects. I. Goodwin, Tony, 1962- II. Title.
  HD38.2.O44 2010
  338.092'2--dc22
                     2010020221

Typeset by Saxon Graphics Ltd, Derby
Printed and bound in Great Britain by
MPG Books Ltd, Bodmin, Cornwall

Contents

About the Authors

Journalist **Jamie Oliver** has written for a number of national newspapers in the United Kingdom, most notably the *Financial Times* and the *Daily Telegraph*. He has written for business and consumer magazines in the United Kingdom and beyond, concentrating on entrepreneurship and business. He has interviewed a range of high-flying entrepreneurs over the past 15 years, including Starbucks founder Howard Schultz, Chinese tycoon David Tang and UK advertising guru Martin Sorrell. He's written about everything from philanthropy to art dealers, blueberries to stuntmen. Researching and writing this book, though, has probably been the most illuminating of all his work to date, teaching him, and he hopes readers, much more about the reality behind business and entrepreneurship than any glossy magazine profile piece.

www.jamieoliverjournalist.com

Tony Goodwin is a successful entrepreneur who has run his own recruitment business for 17 years in territories around the world, from Russia to China, the Middle East to Africa. He has suffered through three major recessions, one of which (between 2001 and 2003) brought his business close to collapse and forced him to seek creditor protection. Since then, Goodwin has ploughed back his life savings and all his worldly assets to save the company. Five years on, he sold his Russian business for many tens of millions of dollars.

He has set up a business, almost lost the lot but come out the other side. The business experiences gives him a particular insight and understanding of what it takes to build an entrepreneurial business – and how that business can come close to disaster.

www.antal.com

Introduction

Hard work, success, wealth, investments, fast cars, country houses, private jets, yachts, pretty wives.

Debt, mounting worries, fear, court proceedings, death threats, bankruptcy, prison, suicide, solitary confinement.

It is a very fine line.

To succeed in business entrepreneurs require courage, they need to be able to take risks, they need a vision, and they must have complete confidence in themselves and their abilities. To fail in business, that courage becomes foolhardiness, the risks become disproportionate, the vision loses focus and the confidence becomes arrogance. And there is not a lot between the two.

This book is about entrepreneurs and the leaders of some of the world's greatest business failures. It is about how they went from hero to zero – and how they managed to blow it in the most spectacular manner possible. And from the failures, this book aims to highlight some of the lessons all entrepreneurs and business leaders can learn.

From unimaginable riches to languishing in a Siberian prison; from heading up one of Wall Street's most successful investment banks to facing stinging criticism from a US House Committee. One way or another, they all blew it. We look at how and why.

This book is about people, about the central human element at the heart of these business catastrophes. It is about entre-preneurs and business leaders, and what drives these people to succeed and then to fail. Often, it is the same thing. And it often ends in tragedy.

Three of the people in this book are dead. Ken Lay had a heart attack and died facing charges surrounding his criminal role in the bankruptcy of the once-mighty Enron Corporation. Adolf Merckle, the German industrialist and multi-billionaire, lost a fortune and stepped in front of a train aged 74. British businessman Christopher Foster killed his dogs, horses, daughter and wife, before setting his house on fire and dying of smoke inhalation. These were tragic ends to incredibly successful careers.

Others in the book sit in prison. Bernie Ebbers from WorldCom, inmate 56022-054, currently resides in the Oakdale Federal Correctional Institution in Oakdale, Louisiana. Russian oligarch Mikhail Khodorkovsky finds himself in a Siberian prison, and Chinese property developer Zhou Zhengyi is also behind bars in Shanghai. Others simply lost vast fortunes. Yet it is never simple.

All sorts of people, friends, family, employees, suppliers and associates will have suffered also at the hands of the 16 men featured in this book. Good news for the lawyers, bad news for everyone else.

Entrepreneurs are many things. They have many admi-rable, likeable and worthy characteristics. Many of those in this book do or did a lot of good work for charities or society at large. WorldCom's Bernie Ebbers taught Sunday school classes in Brookhaven, Mississippi; Guy Naggar supported a series of artistic institutions. Even Dick 'the gorilla' Fuld, more business leader than entrepreneur, of course, was on the board of directors of the Robin Hood Foundation, a charitable organization which tackles poverty in New York City.

But these leaders also have traits that do not endear. While there is no doubt that some entrepreneurs cross the line into criminality, the vast majority do not set out to deceive, defraud or steal money. They set out to build something, to achieve something and to grow something.

Yet there is a clear line between doing business fairly, legally and properly, and trading while knowingly insolvent, or selling shoddy goods or services for vastly inflated prices. Some of those in the book crossed that line: Bernie Ebbers, Reuben Singh and Ken Lay to name just three.

This book is about entrepreneurs, not fraudsters. That is why it has avoided including the likes of disgraced former US financier Bernard Madoff.

There are no end of books on corporate success and a myriad of self-help books: how this product became the world's best seller; how that person made his career defining decisions which produced billions in revenues; why taking a particular path in life was staggeringly successful for the author or subject of the biography. Of course people want to know how other people have done it and if the success can be replicated. Yet often the reader is left with a feeling that they do not really know how they did it, or that certain events, facts, difficulties and challenges were not included in the book. Were they really just friendly, inspiring people?

Surely the best way to learn is from mistakes and it has been said that the definition of intelligence lies not in making mistakes, poor decisions or bad judgments – it lies in not repeating them. And that is what this book sets out to cover.

This book's aim is positive. By examining some of the world's most prolific and successful businessmen and entrepreneurs, and looking at their falls from grace, the idea is to learn lessons about how to avoid those mistakes.

Iranian entrepreneur Robert Tchenguiz built up an incredibly successful business portfolio that concentrated on property and leisure. With property prices ever rising and more money than ever being spent on leisure time, what could go wrong?

British investor Kevin Leech put his earnings into a bewildering array of interests. From cars to computer games, he was the ultimate business angel, sticking in his money to launch or really create a business. Dotcoms were on the rise; it was easy money.

Jón Ásgeir Jóhannesson, the Icelandic retail tycoon, almost single-handedly helped his native country go from a relatively obscure rock in the middle of the Atlantic Ocean to a business colossus on the world stage. Move over Wall Street, the Icelanders are coming!

They all did something remarkable – they all built huge business empires worth billions (at least on paper). But then they all did something unbelievable – they somehow managed to lose it. They blew it. They had it, now they don't.

This is not a witch hunt – the facts are there for all to see. The idea is to present the facts, pick through the bones of what happened in each case, and try to provide lessons to other would-be entrepreneurs. Ultimately, the failings were mostly very human ones. Pride, envy, greed, hubris and ego were never far away in many of the cases, but there was more to it than that. It takes some effort to lose a billion dollars.

The credit crunch and associated recession wiped something like £155 billion from the fortunes of Britain's richest 1,000 people, according to the *Sunday Times Rich List*. That is equivalent to more than a third of their wealth. The *Forbes* magazine rich list of billionaires has seen 332 names cut from the list, and those left have lost around 23 per cent of their wealth. The likes of Bernie Ebbers and Ken Lay, once gracing the world's rich lists are doing so no more.

But rather than bringing into question the capitalist system, the ongoing economic issues have intensified its justification. The period has witnessed families, corporations and generational dynasties being razed to the ground by the credit crisis, poor decision making, bad management, gambling and sometimes pure fraud.

It shows there is no members club of unassailable wealth; no rich man's conspiracy to which the man in the street does not belong. This meritocratic wealth evaporation is a form of socialist capitalism. No one is immune from ruin, no one is spared from the tsunami of bankruptcies that have spread from coast to coast, across national boundaries and permeated even the most hallowed, revered bastions of capitalism.

It proves the thesis of capitalism: it respects no one and does not discriminate in favour of or against race, colour, ethnicity, gender or religion – or the previous size of a bank balance. If you fly too close to the sun, just like Icarus, you will fall into the sea.

Speaking of that, imagine yourself on a transatlantic boat race, having left from Southampton, England. Exactly half way across the Atlantic, your million-dollar catamaran capsizes. You manage to get on board a rowing boat, perhaps with a few other crew members or maybe alone. What do you do? Row back to England or continue to the United States? It is the sort of no-win situation faced by entrepreneurs. A business they have built up for 5, 10 or 20 years is facing bankruptcy. They are faced with putting up more money – their personal money, not the bank's – into their business or letting it capsize. After all the years of building their business brand and reputation they have a tough call. But it's not just about them. There are long-term staff working at the business who are now firm family friends. What do they do?

Most entrepreneurs end up putting a large part, and in most cases all, of the money they have accumulated, their entire wealth, on the line to save the business. Mark Goldberg is a great example. They have to do this because no one else will do it and they cannot bear to see their 'baby' die.

It is not something people who have not run a business can easily understand.

Often, the entrepreneur is perceived as wily, shrewd, in it for themselves, self-serving and never making a decision that will impair their financial position. And for most of their business lives this is probably a reasonable appraisal of their character and situation. Yet faced with bankruptcy, the entrepreneurial attitude can change completely. From being analytically shrewd, intuitive and calculating, they become emotional, generous and illogical. Again, Goldberg, with his blind love for Crystal Palace Football Club, is a prime example.

That is normally the point at which they decide to put far too much of their own money back into the business, or pledge far too many personal guarantees to banks and more dubious lenders in a fraught and desperate bid to save their prized business from impending doom.

This tale of last-ditch attempts to resolve a disintegrating business is repeated many times in this book. Adolf Merckle, the German industrialist, took a bet on the share price of car manufacturer Porsche and he got it wrong. He lost billions and took his own life as a result. James Cayne at Bear Stearns, even in the final dying days of the US investment bank, was counting on pulling off one final deal to save the day. It didn't happen. Bernie Ebbers, the self-confessed technophobe, was on the verge of buying his firm's rival Sprint Communications for a staggering US $115 billion just as the wheels were coming off his business. It was all or nothing for all three men.

All the people featured in this book are male. Indeed, it would have been a difficult task to make it all female. In a way this is understandable – there are simply more men heading large businesses who are in a position to blow it. The former British deputy prime minister, Harriet Harman, even went as far to say that if there were more women at the top of big businesses, the credit crunch might not have occurred at all. If Lehman Brothers was Lehman Sisters, who knows?

But with more and more women running businesses around the world, there must be more to it than that. So why do no women feature? It might be something to do with legacy – and the propensity to take risk.

British King Henry VIII is a great example of a man desperate to leave a legacy. By the time he died in 1547 he had more than 60 houses, yet it was Hampton Court Palace that was most important to him. Over a 10-year period, he spent more than £62,000 rebuilding and extending the palace (around £18 million in today's money), including tennis courts, bowling alleys, a hunting park of more than 1,100 acres and kitchens covering 36,000 square feet. Construction began on some of his palaces as he was coming to the end of his life, but what better way to show the world what a great and illustrious man he was, what a visionary, what a thinker, what a powerful person he was. Since Henry struggled to bear a son, it was a way of leaving a lasting mark on the world, like kings throughout history. This book features a lot of that attitude.

Yet while a man's needs may inspire him to start his own business and improve his circumstances, this is not what drives a millionaire to become a billionaire or a billionaire to become a multi-billionaire.

Perhaps men put greater store in their business achievements and therefore take more risks than women. Perhaps it is sheer ego. While the female approach is to build a stable business that can support her and her family, the often irrational, nonsensical risk-taking method of growing a business seems very much a male preserve.

But women were there in the background, supporting their husbands, no doubt praying they would find an answer to their current business woes and manage to somehow deal their way out of trouble. Of course, there are many women left to pick up the pieces.

Tied up with this yearning to leave a mark are often relationships with political elites. In most countries, leaving a real mark on the world can only happen with the consent of the government, and woe betide anyone who doubts the power wielded at the top.

Russian businessmen Boris Berezovsky and Mikhail Khodorkovsky are two great examples of entrepreneurs getting close – too close – to the powers that be. Berezovsky, a former oil baron, once had the ear of a Russian prime minister: he's now in exile in the United Kingdom, the target of death threats and various attempts on his life. Khodorkovsky, once the 16th wealthiest man on the planet, now languishes in a Siberian prison, scolded for not attending sewing classes. Both wanted more – they had money but they wanted real political influence. It is a dangerous game.

It is also odd, knowing the risks, that they would wish to become embroiled with the murky world of politics. Numerous other successful business people and entrepreneurs, the likes of Bill Gates (Microsoft), the Walton family (WalMart) and in the United Kingdom figures such as Charles Dunstone (Carphone Warehouse) and John Caudwell (founder of Phones4u), have avoided being overtly involved with politics. Some business people appear to be seduced by the power of politics, others realize it's best left well alone. Ultimately, politicians and political parties come and go – getting involved too deep with either side can lead to disaster.

Apple founder Steve Jobs said there's no point being the richest man in the cemetery. He's right, of course, and religious scriptures from around the world have long reiterated the point that you can't take your earthly wealth with you. Yet enough often doesn't seem to be enough for the super-rich. Guy Naggar and Peter Klimt, two men who ran one of Europe's most successful property portfolios, got into all sorts of businesses and ventures. Rich beyond most people's imagination, with art collections that would make most galleries blush, they too wanted more: the next deal, the next profit.

Building a fortune for the next generation is fraught with problems. Newspapers are full of wealthy second or third generations squandering away the hard-earned fortunes, children reduced to drug addicts, dysfunctional and squabbling over the remains. So why do so many entrepreneurs pursue the sort of wealth that they could never possibly spend? Why are they never satisfied with what they have? Why do they want more?

It is here that there is a distinct difference between so-called ordinary people and entrepreneurs. Research has shown that when people earn more than £300,000 (US $480,000) annually, their behaviour changes. Quality of life issues, such as spending more time with the children, become more important.

Yet the entrepreneurs in this book earned considerably more than £300,000 and few showed any sign of letting up. Adolf Merckle was worth close to US$13 billion when he gambled on the stock market – he lost billions, but not his entire fortune. It was enough to send him over the edge. Was he continuing to pursue this high-risk strategy to further improve his already privileged and extremely luxurious position? The man regularly rode to work on a bike and drove a battered old car, so it's doubtful. Far more likely are the more noble of human emotions and motivations – respect, admiration and self-realization.

These people, these entrepreneurs, are relentless.

Many wealthy people look to sport as a way of spending their money. Bernie Ebbers bought a minor league hockey team in Mississippi. Perhaps those who do this want the thrill of success that they can rarely share in their business lives. Entrepreneurship, after all, can be a lonely business.

Investing in a football club proved to be the undoing on one of the entrepreneurs in this book, British millionaire Mark Goldberg. He invested his entire fortune into a London club only to see the thing collapse around his ears. While he cracked the IT recruitment business to make his fortune, those skills could not be transferred into making money in sport.

Parallels can be drawn between sportspeople and entrepreneurs, though, particularly in terms of being relentless and having a will to win. No one criticized British rower Steve Redgrave for attempting to win five Olympic gold medals. No one tried to stop US swimmer Michael Phelps going for eight. No one wants Swiss tennis maestro Roger Federer to stop playing tennis even though he's won so many grand slams titles. So why should the likes of Robert Tchenguiz, Kevin Leech and Reuben Singh stop trying to make more money? It is what they do, after all.

There is an argument that some entrepreneurs are driven by insecurity and a desire to prove themselves. While the monstrous egos and extravagant lifestyles are there for all to see, it is often a deep-seated insecurity or a desire to prove themselves that are at the real root of the entrepreneurial drive. Many of those included in this book came from humble backgrounds: Bernie Ebbers' father was a travelling salesman and Kevin Leech's father ran a garage. It is understandable that they would want to better themselves and once they had, not return to those roots.

On the other hand some of those in this book had wealthy families and cosseted upbringings. Robert Tchenguiz's father was a wealthy businessman. These men had it all on a plate, but either than plate wasn't big enough or they wanted a big plate of their own. In principle, there is nothing wrong with this.

The book also looks at a number of supposedly deeply religious men. They went to church, prayed regularly, donated to good causes and helped those less well off in their communities. Ken Lay and Bernie Ebbers were big religious believers, using God in their defence, citing God as their Maker, the one and only being who could judge them. Of course, in a way, they were wrong. They were both judged by their fellow men and found guilty.

It is hard to see how they could have truly believed in God and the teachings of Christianity, and allowed the wrongdoing in their businesses to continue. In Lay's case, he allowed Enron finance chief Jeff Skilling to cook the books and other senior executives to get away with other lurid behaviour that would have been an instantly sackable offence in most other businesses. Yet while the money was being made, Lay turned a blind eye. Is that what it says to do in the Bible?

More bizarre still was the fact that Bernie Ebbers taught Sunday school classes. Today's lesson: Thou shalt not steal…

Somewhere down the road, these business people crossed a line. It is difficult to pick out one defining point at which these people changed. While efforts have been made to present a balanced view on what took place in these case studies, the truth is, only the men at the top will ever really know what went on and at which point the writing was on the wall. Some, of course, remain unrepentant. Ken Lay went to his grave talking up his innocence. Others have taken – or will take – their secrets with them.

The fact is that life is complicated, and business life even more so. Human motivation, emotion, politics, bias and subjectivity cloud and mystify even the most basic profit-driven transactions. What seems like a simple business model invariably isn't. What seems like a straightforward deal is anything but once the volatility, urges and mood swings of the main protagonists are taken into account. That is the point of this book: to look at the facts, and look at the people at the heart of these incredible business collapses.

Just how did these people manage to blow it?

Chapter One

Bernie Ebbers
– Chosen?

Whether Bernie Ebbers really believed he was chosen by God, as he once claimed, we will never know. But by the end of the 1990s, he could be forgiven for thinking he had indeed been anointed. He had grown WorldCom into a business worth billions, he had a pretty young wife, and he graced the covers of magazines. Yet within a few years, the company admitted to massive accounting misstatements, 20,000 workers lost their jobs, and shareholders lost about US$180 billion. In the final reckoning, it certainly was a catastrophe of biblical proportions.

Bernard J Ebbers was born in Edmonton, Canada, the second of five children. His father was a travelling salesman and while he was growing up he also lived in California and New Mexico, before returning to Edmonton. He briefly attended the University of Alberta and Calvin College, then took jobs working as a milkman and bouncer, before enrolling at Mississippi College. There he earned a basketball scholarship, and in 1967 he achieved a bachelor's degree in physical education, with a minor in secondary education. He settled in Mississippi, and a year later he married Linda Pigott. They had three daughters. By the high American educational and standards, it was a very modest start to life.

Ebbers' first foray into business was operating a chain of hotels in Mississippi, and by 1981 he and some business associates ran nine hotels. It was around this time that the US authorities started de-monopolizing national telephone communications, meaning anyone could rent a communication channel from the likes of AT&T or other big carriers and transmit long-distance calls. One of Ebbers' hotels obtained the right to rent one of Mississippi's telephone lines, and it gave Bernie the idea he'd been looking for. One evening, sat talking to friends in the Days Inn coffee shop in Hattiesburg, Mississippi, Ebbers came up with a scheme to buy long-distance communication from Southern Central Bell and then resell it to local enterprises. By 1983, the friends founded Long Distance Discount Service (LDDS). Two years later, Ebbers was chief executive.

It was a genuine entrepreneurial, eureka moment – and Ebbers needs to be given full credit. Great and successful entrepreneurs share this common trait: the vision necessary to build really great and sustainable companies. The big difference is that those who continue to be a success remain focused on what they are good at. Ebbers did not.

To say Ebbers was an outsider when it came to the telecoms industry is something of an understatement. Never happier than when riding a tractor, so he said, Ebbers was always a technophobe, rarely using e-mail and hardly ever sitting down at a computer. Yet here he was about to embark on one of the most dazzling telecoms acquisitions trails the United States and the world had ever seen.

This lack of industry knowledge is surprisingly common in successful entrepreneurs, and there are all manner of examples of people succeeding despite their shortage of industry know-how. British mobile phone billionaire John Caudwell, founder of Phones4u, famously sold second-hand cars before going into the telecoms business.

In 1985 Ebbers became president of LDDS, and the company started buying up small long-distance companies in the south and west of the United States. Deals for Metromedia Communications, Resurgens Communications Group, and IDB Communications Group in 1993 and 1994 put the company into markets in the northeast, California and Europe. Ebbers the dealmaker was in his element. Within 10 years LDDS had acquired more than 60 independent telecoms firms, and in 1995 it changed its name to WorldCom.

The relentless deal making continued. In 1996 WorldCom acquired MFS Communications, a company that lets large businesses connect their voice and data calls to long-distance networks without using the local phone company or paying access charges. It had recently acquired UUNet and its internet capacity. At the time, the US$12.5 billion transaction was one of the largest corporate acquisitions in US history.

The combination of acquisitions allowed Ebbers to control long distance, local service and data communications – and the numbers made for spectacular reading. In 1996, operating income reached US$896.1 million on revenues of US$5.6 billion. The company expected revenues to grow in that year alone by an additional 23 per cent to US$6.9 billion.

Ebbers was shaking up the cosy world of telecoms – but he was not finished yet. Early in the morning on 1 October 1997, the audacious Ebbers picked up the phone in a New York hotel and called Bert Roberts, the chief executive officer of MCI Communications Corp. Roberts hadn't arrived in the office. Ebbers reportedly called back at 8.30 am and told Roberts that WorldCom (with revenues of US$5.6 billion) was making an unsolicited bid for MCI (with revenues of US$18.5 billion). To rub it in, Ebbers later joked with reporters that if Roberts winds up working for him, he'd better be in the office 'a little bit earlier'.

MCI had been in discussion with BT at the time about a possible deal, but Ebbers was not concerned. 'After we get our deal done with MCI,' said the cocksure Canadian, 'we may acquire BT.' WorldCom's successful acquisition of MCI, offering US$30 billion in stock and the assumption of US$5 billion in debt, was completed in September 1998. The telecoms industry was in shock.

The business community, especially in Mississippi, flocked to praise Ebbers. He was inducted into the Mississippi Business Hall of Fame in May 1995 'because of his commitment to developing jobs and resources in Mississippi's telecommunications industry', and the MetroJackson Chamber of Commerce named WorldCom 'Business of the Year' for 1998. He received Mississippi College's highest honour, the Alumnus of the Year award, and was granted an honorary Doctor of Laws degree. In 1998, Ebbers was granted an honorary doctorate from the Jackson, Mississippi-based Tougaloo College.

Politicians too flocked to praise Ebbers, with even President Bill Clinton once calling him 'the symbol of 21st century America', adding that Ebbers was 'the embodiment of what I want for the future'.

The business media, meanwhile, was almost universally blinded by the numbers. A US$37 billion merger, more than 22 million customers, 75,000 employees – wow! *Business Week* magazine, on 13 October 1997, featured Ebbers on the front cover and lauded him as the Telecom Cowboy. Little did it know then how close it was to the truth.

Business Week was not the only magazine guilty of building up the cult of Ebbers, although its journalists might think in retrospect that some of their comments were rather rash. 'Ebbers is now showing industry veterans what the new era in communications is all about', it puffed in 1997. *Forbes*, *Financial World*, *Fortune* and *Inc.* magazines all chimed in with celebratory pieces, and Ebbers was presented with a variety of accolades. The award-winning Salon.com compared the rise of Bernie Ebbers 'with the rise of the industrial tycoons of the 19th century'. It said, 'Ebbers is the servant of his shareholders', adding that 'we live in a far more rational, and arguably more honest, economic world'. That is arguable indeed.

All the talk was of WorldCom being a 21st-century telecoms company, and of Ebbers being the 'unconventional' cowboy, riding to the industry's rescue. Shareholder return was the key, paying careful attention to share prices. Earnings potential ruled, and it was mentioned how Ebbers' interests and his shareholders' were completely 'aligned'.

While we all know what's coming, Ebbers' insatiable hunger for acquisitions showed no sign of abating: not a bit of it. Next on the agenda was the mother of all deals. In 1999, Ebbers announced that MCI WorldCom would attempt to acquire its rival Sprint Communications for a staggering US$115 billion.

While it is one thing buying up small Mississippi-based telecoms firms, it is on an altogether different plateau when the amount you are offering for a company is more than the entire GDP of countries such as Bulgaria, Ecuador and New Zealand. The project was soon abandoned in the wake of objections by US and EU regulators, but that was just the start of WorldCom's and Ebbers' woes.

A downturn in the telecom market soon put paid to any other grand acquisition plans – and it rapidly had a devastating impact on WorldCom and, by extension, Ebbers. From a peak in 1999 of US$64.50, by the time Ebbers resigned in 2002, the WorldCom share price had fallen to just US$1.79. For an acquisitions spree built on the value of the stock-price, that was not good.

While much press coverage up to this point had been positive, questioning voices were out there (although these were often scoffed at in other media). The *New York Times*, for example, said Ebbers surely had to slow down on buying corporations and 'learn to run what he has built'. But do deal junkies ever really learn to run what they have built? While history has notable exceptions, such as Sir Martin Sorrell at WPP, Gerald Ronson at Heron International and the late Lord Weinstock at GEC Marconi, there are plenty more who appear only interested in the deal. Many of these gallivanting entrepreneurs never give the impression that they are ever running their businesses or sticking to what they are good at. Perhaps what they are good at is the deal. But many come unstuck as a result.

In April 1999, while *Network World* magazine called Ebbers one of the '25 most powerful people in networking', it did strike a note of caution that would be eerily prescient. It noted that Ebbers had never completely integrated the acquisitions of MFS, Brooks and UUNET before swallowing MCI, and stated that he would need to turn MCI WorldCom 'into a complete, wrinkle-free package'.

At his 'peak' in early 1999, Ebbers was estimated to be worth US$1.4 billion, putting him at number 174 on the Forbes 400. While he was the classic corporate shopaholic, his personal acquisitions trail is no less impressive. In 1998 he purchased Douglas Lake, which at 500,000 acres is Canada's biggest ranch (for US$14 million), a lumber mill in Brookhaven,

Mississippi and a livestock farm in Mississippi, and in 1999 he bought Joshua Timberlands, 540,000 acres of lumber land in Mississippi, Tennessee, Louisiana and Alabama for about US$600 million. He also bought a minor league hockey team in Mississippi.

There often appears to be a desire in men, as opposed to women, to leave their DNA footprint on the world. There are similar stories throughout history of important men, the likes of Henry VIII, who have a penchant for building palaces that will clearly outlive their mortal bodies. In business there are similarly grandiose dreams: the purchasing of disparate, unconnected assets and businesses in the vain hope that the legacy will be continued.

For Ebbers, there had been seven major purchases in two years, any one of which would have represented the realization of a life-long dream for a normal person. So why was he driven to such material gluttony? Was it just ego and pure greed? We think not. This is empire building beyond ego, rationale and conscious thought: it has to be driven by something much deeper and more instinctive.

The cowboy moniker was no doubt accurate, and Ebbers sauntered through the corporate headquarters in Jackson, Mississippi, in faded jeans while 'chomping on a cigar'. But there are parallels between his corporate spending sprees and his personal ones – and some of the same failings are there in both. For one, he had a tendency to overpay – not only for telecoms firms at the height of the telecoms boom, but also in terms of his personal purchases. The US$65 million he spent on his British Columbia ranch was said to have been US$15 million too much. The US$14 million he spent to buy Intermarine, along with the US$25 million he then invested, was another questionable investment.

Some of his personal investments were made as a result of friendship and loyalty rather than pure business acumen, something that can be linked in part to his religious faith. It was a big factor in Ebbers' life, and he is even said to have opened corporate meetings with prayer. A member of the Easthaven Baptist Church in Brookhaven, Mississippi, Ebbers occasionally taught in the Sunday school, as unbelievable as it may sound today. And it is interesting to note that when allegations against him first came out that he addressed the congregation and said, 'I just want you to know you aren't going to church with a crook.' He also once said: 'I believe God has a plan for people's lives, and I believe he had a plan for me.' And what a plan!

On 25 June 2002, WorldCom admitted to US$3.85 billion in accounting misstatements. The figure ultimately grew to US$11 billion – and all roads lead to Ebbers. He appeared before the US House Committee on Financial Services on 8 July 2002, and made the following statement: 'I do not believe I have anything to hide, I believe that no one will conclude that I engaged in any criminal or fraudulent conduct.' And with that, he promptly asserted his Fifth Amendment right against self-incrimination. He couldn't have been more wrong.

With Ebbers sitting mute, the committee had a difficult time getting answers. They were incredulous, though, that the fraud only came to light thanks to a WorldCom vice president, Cynthia Cooper, working with a small team, when accounting firm Authur Andersen somehow managed to miss it after it had spent 15 months and 15,000 employee hours looking into the case. There were many more hours to come.

One theme will recur again: financial, audit, governance and control institutions did not cover themselves in glory.

When US federal authorities came to indict Ebbers on 2 March 2004, the charges were clear: one count each of conspiracy and securities fraud, and seven counts of filing false statements with securities regulators. Despite protestations of innocence, calls for leniency on account of his charitable work and pleas for clemency because of an apparent heart condition, federal judge Barbara Jones was unmoved. She rejected his lawyers' contention that Ebbers was not a mastermind of the accounting wrong-doing. Ebbers, she said, 'was clearly a leader of criminal activity in this case'. He was found guilty of all charges on 15 March 2005, and on 13 July Judge Jones sentenced Ebbers to a staggering 25 years in a federal prison in Louisiana, the longest stretch ever handed down in the history of corporate America.

Ebbers wept. He self-reported to Oakdale Federal Correctional Institution in Oakdale, Louisiana on 26 September 2006, a low-security prison he happens to share with Andrew Fastow, the former chief financial officer for Enron Corporation. He drove himself to prison in his Mercedes and is serving his sentence as inmate #56022-054. The earliest date he can be released is in July 2028, by when he will be more than 85 years old.

So what went wrong? Whistleblower Cynthia Cooper, the internal auditor from WorldCom who first uncovered the black hole in the accounts, says neither the fraud nor the discovery of the fraud caused the downfall. It goes deeper than that. She blames the state of the market, the falling stock price, loading the company with debt and 'poor decisions when it came to acquisitions'.

Former US attorney general Richard Thornburgh, appointed by the bankruptcy court to study WorldCom's failure, agreed that the many acquisitions were poorly integrated and that strategic planning, headed by Ebbers, was especially weak. Basically, Ebbers used WorldCom stock to pull off acquisitions. Thornburgh concluded that Ebbers used WorldCom shares to secure more than US$1 billion in personal and business loans.

While there had been some words of caution in the media, they had been few and far between. *Networking World* did suggest (at the same time as awarding Ebbers yet another accolade, so he might have missed the slight criticism) that he should concentrate on what he was supposed to be doing. But he chose not to heed the magazine's advice – nor seemingly to listen to any advice from cautious advisors – if there were any.

Ebbers was operating on a grand scale, and he was certainly guilty of lacking attention to detail. He missed the 'miracle of the mundane' that epitomizes some of the world's best businesses such as Wal-Mart, Tesco and Apple. These businesses focus on the minutiae of their business model relentlessly, and their customers love them for it. Even when times are tough, the customers keep on coming.

Former WorldCom associates said that when using his stock as collateral, on its seemingly endless upward trajectory, Ebbers felt that it was essentially 'free'. It was to make him and break him. When the stock price went south, lenders who accepted stock as collateral started calling in loans. Cue the book cooking.

The idea that Ebbers had access to 'free money' is an interesting concept – it simply does not exist. Yet there are many examples of business people lulled by their own success into feeling that they are somehow the treasury of a national government. They think they are printing money and that they have power over it. It's a similar situation with some governments. Senior treasury ministers the world over appear to believe that tax money belongs to them. Most come unstuck.

Ultimately, it is the people who know most about the value of money, about profit margins, the costs of things and the power of negotiation, who have the best credentials for a great entrepreneurial career. When they begin to lose this control, this understanding, then they begin their descent – maybe imperceptibly at first, but surely enough. And Ebbers certainly descended.

SOURCES

Business Week, October 1997

Clarion Ledger, July 2002

CNN Money, March 2004

Finance Conference 2000, the new economy, http://www.bc.edu/bc_org/mvp/fincon/ebbers.html

Findlaw, First Interim Report of Dick Thornburgh, bankruptcy court examiner, November 2002: http://news.corporate.findlaw.com/hdocs/docs/worldcom/thornburgh1strpt.pdf

Portfolio.com, The worst American CEOs of all time, www.cnbc.com/id/30502091/

Network World, April 1999

Thesalon.com, October 2006

Thestreet.com, March 2008

Time magazine, September 1999

US Department of Justice, March 2004

US Federal Bureau of Prisons

USA Today, 11 December 2002

Wired magazine, November 1999

Other sources include BBC, *Financial Times*, *Daily Telegraph*

Chapter Two

Christopher Foster
– Deadly Intent

Christopher Foster's last act was to get into bed with his dead wife Jill. She was dead because he had shot her in the head. As well as his own wife of 21 years, Foster had shot dead his 15-year-old daughter, Kirstie, in her bedroom. At 3.10 am, he then used his .22 rifle to shoot dead the family's dog and horses, before setting fire to the stables. After this, he calmly proceeded to pour 200 gallons of oil into his five-bedroom country home, Osbaston House, near Maesbrook in Shropshire, England. Foster drove his horsebox to the gates of the property, making any attempt at entry difficult for the emergency services. Just to make sure, he shot out the tyres. He then lit the fire, went upstairs and got into bed. He died of smoke inhalation.

The first anyone outside knew of what was unfolding was when ADT Security received a fault message on Foster's alarm system at 3.44 am, indicating something was wrong with the alarm in the library. There was no answer when

ADT tried to call. Soon all the alarms were going off, and at 3.51 am the power went off completely. Meanwhile, neighbours reported hearing shots and explosions coming from the property.

Around the same time, the fire service received a 999 call for a reported fire at Osbaston House. When they and the police arrived on the scene, the scale of the blaze took them by surprise. That someone had put a horsebox at the gates and shot out the tyres indicated that whoever had started the fire did not want it to be put out. It took 12 fire crews several days to contain the flames. The police were forced to stand and watch as vital evidence went up in smoke. 'It was like a clay oven turning everything to ash,' said Detective Superintendent Jon Groves who led the investigation.

At first, speculation was rife about what had taken place and why. But when the police made it clear they were not looking for anyone else in relation to the incident, it became apparent that they were dealing with a tragedy. And when Foster's own CCTV footage was looked through, it was clear what had taken place.

The police found Chris and Jill's bodies by accident, while taking forensic pictures. They were revealed to have fallen through the burned floor from above while still entwined. A loaded rifle, complete with silencer, was recovered from near his body.

Friends and relatives were shocked and horrified that Foster could have done such a thing. 'I think what Chris Foster did was the most despicable thing I've ever had to deal with,' said forensics officer Dominic Black in a newspaper interview. 'As a father, he had been put on this planet to protect that girl. She was in her own home, in her own bedroom, with her own parents. The safest place in the world for anybody and he takes her life. That fills me with horror.'

The coroner's inquest confirmed what the police had deduced. Firearms expert Phillip Rydeard told the coroner that the recovered gun was a German-made .22 bolt-action rifle. He also confirmed that the three fragments of lead recovered from Jill Foster's skull were consistent with having been fired from the weapon. And the wound in Kirstie's skull was typical of a gunshot. It was a nightmare.

Quite how Foster could have turned a gun on his own wife and daughter we shall never know. Perhaps even harder to take for friends and family is that only hours beforehand, the family had enjoyed a day's clay pigeon shooting and barbecue. A photograph from the party, showing a smiling Christopher, Jill and Kirstie, was published soon after the incident. There was no sign of the impending tragedy. John Hughes, who hosted the event, said that during the day Foster seemed in very good spirits. But while Jill and Kirstie wanted to stay, Christopher was insistent that they left early. He already knew what was coming.

Guests from the barbeque do recall Foster mentioning that 'Russians owed him money', but no one thought anything of it. In reality, Foster's business dealings had been on a downward trajectory for some time.

Christopher Foster came from fairly humble roots. His father was said to have sold mattresses door to door in Blackpool, while Foster's own first job was as an apprentice electrician. His and Jill's first home was a suburban new build in Wolverhampton, a metropolitan borough of the West Midlands in England. He went on to become an insulation salesman, but it was while watching the unfolding Piper Alpha oil platform disaster that he had his eureka moment. The event prompted Foster to invent a new type of insulation that could protect the valves on oil platforms from being destroyed. Oil firms showed interest, but wanted proof that it worked. So he remortgaged his house, purchased £5,000 worth of gas to use in the demonstration, and according to his mother, Enid, stood there with his fingers crossed as the fire raged. After the flames died down, the values were untouched. His product, UlvaShield, worked.

This was Foster the entrepreneur. He did what few professional people would do, remortgaged his house for an idea that he had no guarantee would work. Up to this point, no one had backed him; no one supported him. The bank only loaned money it knew it would get back. Foster was on his own. It was his finest moment. It is just a pity he could not exercise such judgement and character throughout the rest of his business career.

Foster set up Ulva Ltd in 1998, based in Rugeley, Staffordshire, and the following year he managed to secure a £500,000 export deal with backing from British Trade International to supply thermal insulation for Petro-Canada, a Canadian oil company. Foster's company was soon turning over £1.5 million annually, and he claimed that he was winning every offshore construction project that he targeted in Britain. There was also talk of Ulva winning a lucrative contract to supply insulation to the new 1,100-mile Caspian pipeline, which runs from the Caspian Sea to the Mediterranean, through Azerbaijan and Turkey. It is hard to overestimate the impact a contract like this would have had on the small company. In the multi-billion-dollar oil industry, it would have placed Ulva in the big league.

Foster was at the top of his game. There can be few better moments for entrepreneurs than when the world, however small that world, appears to be taking notice of them and buying their product, service or idea. Making even the smallest amount of money can be vindication for months or years of effort, although in Foster's case, he was raking it in. 'He was making money hand over fist,' said his mother. 'He had so much that he didn't know what to do with it.' It did not take him long.

Apparently Foster's wife Jill first saw Osbaston House up for sale in *Shropshire Life* magazine. That was on a Thursday. They viewed it on Saturday and bought it, with £1 million cash, that very afternoon. Foster was said to have spent another £200,000-plus on antiques and furniture for the property. When the family moved into the property, Foster apparently arrived with two Range Rovers to impress the neighbours. His car collection also included at different times a Bentley, matching 'his and hers' Porsches, a Ferrari, an Aston Martin and a silver Jaguar. He also bought horses for Kirstie, who was sent to the private Ellesmere College, a few miles away. And why not? Foster had worked hard and pulled off an incredible business coup. Why not let the world see the spoils of this effort?

Foster's passion became shooting. Gun ownership is strictly regulated in the United Kingdom, with anyone owning a weapon requiring a licence, or firearm certificate. To obtain a firearm certificate, the police must be convinced that a person has 'good reason' to own each gun, and that they can be trusted with it 'without danger to the public safety or to the peace'. Around 1 million people regularly shoot in the United Kingdom, creating an industry worth around £1.6 billion.

Foster certainly had cause to own weapons. He joined the local gun club, and would shoot up to four days a week. Coming in at some £4,000 per day, it was not cheap. One year he reportedly spent £80,000 on shooting, and he ordered custom-made shotguns from Purdey and Beretta that cost £70,000 and £35,000 respectively. There was no reason to believe that Foster would turn the guns on his own family.

It was not the guns that should have concerned those working with Foster, though. Spending so much time away from a young and growing business was a bad idea, particularly in the case of Ulva when it was on the verge of a real global breakthrough. And it was not just the shooting that was occupying his time.

First, there was a dispute to do with a property deal in Cyprus. In 2006, Foster complained to the police that two men, Tim Baker and Leo Dennis, were attempting to bribe him – a charge they strongly denied. Dennis claimed the bribery accusation was a smokescreen to cover up the fact that Foster had offered him £50,000 to kill his mistress's husband. The lurid claims and counter claims were soon dismissed by Shrewsbury Crown Court and the two were cleared, but it shone a light on the sort of murky business world in which Foster moved – and showed how he had clearly taken his eye off issues at Ulva. Worse was to follow.

Foster's company Ulva had an exclusivity agreement with its main supplier, Cambridge-based DRC Distribution, a subsidiary of the SWP Group. But with his business running into trouble, Foster found a cheaper supplier in the United States. At the same time, DRC was finding it harder and harder to get paid on time. The situation deteriorated when DRC claimed breach of contract and Ulva served notice of termination of the contract. A contractual battle ensued, and by July 2007 the case ended up before the High Court. Ulva accepted that it was in breach of contract, and the judge suggested that 'morally' Ulva was in the wrong, leaving DRC out of pocket but in a position to claim back damages, believed to be around £800,000.

All the time the legal dispute had rumbled on, Foster had been secretly transferring the bulk of Ulva's assets to either himself or a new 'phoenix company', called Ulva Holdings, of which he was the director. On 29 June 2007 Ulva ceased to trade, and when Her Majesty's Revenue & Customs threatened to wind up the company, Foster brought in the administrators.

DRC refused to be fobbed off without payment of the damages due to it, and applied to the court to have Ulva's administrators removed. The Court of Appeal agreed: Foster's scam did not work. Lord Justice Rimmer said that the share transfer deal was 'an asset stripping exercise directed at enabling him to carry on his business through another company with a similar name'. He added that Foster was 'not to be trusted'. In May 2008, the judge ruled that the administrators were jointly liable with Foster for the £800,000 legal costs of DRC. The UK tax authorities were also on Foster's back for unpaid taxes totalling about £1 million.

The most galling aspect of the case for Foster was that Ulva was bought by the SWP Group for a 'nominal' sum. It told investors that Foster's former company offered international 'growth possibilities of transformational proportions', and listed the likes of BP, British Gas and Total as clients.

The final straw for Foster, though, may well have been the legal notice found pinned to the front gates of his Shropshire mansion. Addressed for the attention of Christopher Foster only, it was a legal order stopping Foster and his family from selling the property without authorization from the corporate liquidators.

The game was up. With creditors closing in and talk of dubious Russian business associates, it reached the point where Foster became so paranoid that he started keeping a handgun in his car – which is illegal in the United Kingdom. He also installed high electric gates, and told Belinda, his cleaner, to refuse entry to anyone who was not known to him.

It seems that events were spiralling out of control for Foster, and he apparently believed he had cause to fear for his life. By the end, he had assets of £3.1 million but debts of £4.4 million, including three mortgages on Osbaston House. He told a friend, Mark Bassett, that he would never let any liquidators take his home or possessions away from him, adding, 'I would top myself before that. They would have to carry me out in a box.' They did.

So what sort of man was Foster? For one thing, he obviously had a dark side, and some felt he was very much a Jekyll and Hyde character. While at times charming, he could also be headstrong and impulsive. He would apparently shoot his wife Jill's doves if they got into the garage and left droppings on his car. And more frightening still, he reportedly shot Kirstie's pet Labrador when it worried sheep and the angry farmer threatened to shoot it himself. A man that can shoot his daughter's pet dog! Perhaps the writing was on the wall.

Peter Grkinic, a director of Foster's former company Ulva, said Foster was 'vindictive'. Talking about the threat of his assets being seized, Grkinic said Foster 'took the view that if I can't have it, nobody can have it'.

Foster's GP, Dr William Grech, said that on three occasions in March 2008, Foster told him he was thinking of committing suicide. He said he was not sleeping and was stressed about his business situation. The doctor urged Foster to talk to his wife. He did not. Keith Ashcroft, a forensic psychologist, said his final act 'looks like a man in a state of depression, faced by the threat of his house being repossessed, deciding to take his family's lives to protect them from poverty. That is the fantasy.'

It was a tragic end to a story of promising entrepreneurial endeavour – and it did not have to be like that. Foster acted in a way common to many entrepreneurs who find themselves facing supposedly insurmountable problems. The usual response is to ignore the problems, become a fantasist or simply lie (to others and themselves). The big hope is the entrepreneur can 'deal' their way out of the problems.

In many ways, the characteristics required to become an entrepreneur can end up pushing people over the edge. In the beginning, entrepreneurs are alone, so they have to take themselves very seriously and give themselves an air of credibility. They become very good actors. Foster was a good actor. It is a fine line between bluff and deceit, between confidence and arrogance, between entrepreneur and con man. Entrepreneurs undoubtedly start to believe their own publicity and believe their own hype.

And Foster, looking around at his cars, country squire life-style, horses and shooting, certainly became lulled into a false sense of security. Like many entrepreneurs before him, he took his eye off the ball. Bored by the detail and preferring the upmarket lifestyle, he fell into a trap that a lot of successful entrepreneurs fall into. But the miracle of wealth creation often lies in its mundaneness. Once people lose track of the details, the bigger picture quickly starts to unravel.

The lessons from Foster's tragic story are simple: stick to running what you know and keep doing what works. Foster was sidetracked by the lifestyle, by dubious property deals, and got mixed up with shady people who deflected his attention from what had got him where he was in the first place. He had a great business, which had global potential, but he blew it. Perhaps it was always beyond him. Maybe Christopher Foster rose above his station and simply did not know how to cope. He will not be the last.

SOURCES

DRC Distribution Ltd v *Ulva Ltd* [2007] EWHC 1716, 20 July 2007,
   High Court of Justice (Queen's Bench Division)
Daily Mail, 3 April 2009
Daily Mail, 29 August 2008
Daily Telegraph, 2 April 2009
Daily Telegraph, 3 April 2009
Daily Telegraph, 27 August 2008
Guardian, 4 April 2009
Shropshire Star, 28 August 2008
Sunday Mirror, 31 August 2008
Sunday Times, 31 August 2008
SWP Group plc, www.swpgroupplc.com
The Times, 3 April 2009
The Times, 2 September 2008
ULVA Insulation Systems Ltd, www.ulva.co.uk
www.countryside-alliance.org.uk

Chapter Three

Mikhail Khodorkovsky
– Stitch Up

You do not mess with Vladimir Putin. As Russian president, Putin conducted military offensives, is accused of crushing the opposition and charged with curbing the country's free press. Trained by the KGB, Russia's fearsome former secret service, he has reached the Sixth Dan level in his favourite sport, judo, and has been photographed in recent times variously hunting (with a large weapon), fishing and horse riding (bare chested) and generally looking macho. Most world leaders, if they attempted such things, would be laughing stocks. Picture French leader Nicolas Sarkozy fishing bare-chested.

In Putin's case, the images make the man, and have helped boost his popularity among large portions of the still impoverished Russian population. They point to previous Soviet leaders and say Putin is the best they have had. Putin also has the sort of steely glare that says 'don't mess with me'. And most people do not – or dare not. But occasionally, people have dared to take on Putin, and how they must now wish they had kept schtum.

One such man is Mikhail Borisovich Khodorkovsky. The former head of Yukos, once one of the largest oil producers in the world, he now languishes in a Siberian prison, convicted in 2005 of fraud and sentenced to nine years. In 2008 he was denied parole by Judge Igor Faliliyev, at the Ingodinsky regional court in Chita, Siberia, in part because Khodorkovsky 'refused to attend jail sewing classes'. Even steely-eyed Putin must have smiled momentarily at that one. Welcome to the enigma that is Russia.

Khodorkovsky was born on 26 June 1963, in Moscow. His parents, Boris and Marina, worked as chemical engineers. Khodorkovsky studied chemical engineering, and graduated in 1986 from Moscow's Mendeleev Institute of Chemical Technologies. His dream was to become the manager of a Soviet factory.

It was Khodorkovsky's involvement with the Komsomol, the Communist party's youth organization within the Institute, that really set the direction of his life. Rising to become its deputy chief, he forged friendships and allegiances that would later become critical.

He certainly understood how to get ahead in this theoretically egalitarian environment, and he shares this ability with his fellow entrepreneurs. He knew the best route to success, and in the beginning it was more about privileges and favours than making money. It makes sense that at the fall of communism, the people who knew how to get on in one environment could quickly turn their hands to another, the business of enterprise.

The Komsomol was unusual in that it allowed members to set up enterprises and keep the profits. This fact, along with the economic and political reforms being introduced by

Mikhail Gorbachev, offered opportunities to a few bright and ambitious Russians. And Khodorkovsky was ambitious. Together with some business partners, he started a private cafe, reportedly sold bottles of brandy, and in a world that until then had been starved of widespread access to computer technology, he started buying and selling imported PCs. Business boomed. In two years he was said to have accumulated more than US$1 million. Khodorkovsky, who lists his favourite pastimes as 'listening to Abba records, watching action movies, reading science fiction and pumping iron', was fast becoming something that would have been utterly unthinkable in Russia only a few years previously: a successful entrepreneur.

As the social, political and economic changes in Russia gathered pace, communism fell, Boris Yeltsin came to power, and fleet-footed business people took full advantage. Khodorkovsky and friends used their wealth, as many other people were doing, to set up a bank. Thousands sprang up overnight. Khodorkovsky and his colleagues established Bank Menatep, a privately held banking and financial business, and through Khodorkovsky's friends in high places, it managed to secure lucrative government contracts.

This is yet another example of Khodorkovsky mixing the nitro and glycerine of communist contacts to create capitalistic endeavour. And for a while, it was a success.

The banks that prospered had licences to work in hard currency. Businesses needed dollars to import goods, and banks charged high rates for hard currency. Bank Menatep was authorized to handle the funds of the Ministry of Finance, the State Taxation Service, the Moscow city government and the Russian arms export monopoly. Khodorkovsky, who was also starting to operate internationally, as well as increasingly through off-shore banking affiliates, was getting ever wealthier. But his life was about to change. Back in November 1992, the Russian oil firm Yukos was founded by presidential decree to bring together several state-owned producers. The name Yukos comes from the main producing entities, Siberian oil producer Yuganskneftegaz and Volga refining company KuibyshevnefteOrgSintez. The big time beckoned for Khodorkovsky when Boris Yeltsin started selling off state assets like Yukos in an effort to kick-start the Russian economy.

In December 1995, Bank Menatep was put in charge of processing the bids in the Yukos auction. To no one's surprise, and despite higher bids from rivals (which were rejected for 'technical' reasons), a company run by Bank Menatep and Khodorkovsky won the auction. It is not entirely clear exactly what percentage of the business Khodorkovsky managed to secure (around 78 per cent), nor is it agreed exactly what he paid. Estimates range from US$300 million to US$350 million, with the bank taking on something like US$2 billion in debt. Whatever it was, it was soon looking like the deal of the century. The deal implied a value for the whole company of US$450 million, but when the shares began trading less than two years later, Yukos's market capitalization was US$9 billion. By 2002, it was nearer to US$15 billion.

While in retrospect these deals appear like daylight robbery, the Russian economy in the mid-1990s was in a precarious state. The investment climate today remains relatively risky, and in the few years after the fall of communism it was extremely dubious. There was little political vision, Russia had an unpredictable president, business law was in its infancy and uncertainty was everywhere. It meant that raising money to invest into Russia, even into oil companies, was virtually impossible – and that had an impact on the prices of assets (not to mention the additional issues with favouritism, cronyism and nepotism). Luckily Khodorkovsky was part of the in-crowd.

Even so, from importing computers to controlling Russia's second-largest oil producer, in no time at all, was some achievement for the Muscovite. It put the workaholic Khodorkovsky in an altogether different league, and brought him enormous wealth, great power and considerable influence. It also brought great dangers. In early 1998, Yukos signed an agreement with another major producer, Sibneft, to merge production operations. Sibneft had been acquired for US$100 million in 1996 by Roman Abramovich (who now owns Chelsea Football Club) and Boris Berezovsky (who is now a fugitive from Russian justice). The deal never came off, but the real trouble was just around the corner. In August 1998, Russia defaulted on US$40 billion of its domestic debt and devalued the rouble. The sudden economic meltdown wreaked havoc for financial institutions such as Bank Menatep, leaving it, like Russia itself, close to bankruptcy.

In fact Bank Menatep-Moscow went under, but Khodorkovsky managed to transfer its good accounts to a sister bank called Menatep-St Petersburg. The organization still faced serious problems, not least the angry creditors who were owed US$266 million, secured against Yukos stock. Chief among those were Daiwa Bank and West Merchant Bank, a subsidiary of Westdeutsche Landesbank. Other Western banks also felt the strain. Barclays fell victim to the tune of £250 million, while Credit Suisse First Boston lost the best part of US$1 billion. In Russia, banks literally closed their doors while ordinary citizens queued around the block and fought desperately to save their money. To this day, Russians prefer to keep what money they have under the mattress.

The banks wanted their money back, and refused to listen to Khodorkovsky's three-year repayment plan. In the end, the banks dumped their Yukos shares on the market, getting a fraction of their investment. While some thought this action hasty, it came to light that Yukos was planning to make a share offering that would have seriously diluted the banks' 29 per cent stake. Ultimately, Khodorkovsky and his partners bought back most of the stake themselves.

The Muscovite had a ruthless streak. With its creditors gone, Yukos went from strength to strength. By 2001 it had become the fastest-growing oil company in Russia, and in 2003 it was announced that merger talks were back on with Sibneft. It was even becoming fully legitimate in the eyes of international competitors by its increasingly transparent dealings, culminating in a listing on the New York Stock Exchange. Part of the push to becoming legitimate was down to recruitment policies that encouraged the best and brightest from business schools around the world to work in Russia. There were also steps to lure back expat Russians to the Motherland. Khodorkovsky played a role in this effort, and was said to be personally behind the drive to make Yukos the best-managed oil company in Russia. All this meant that Khodorkovsky's personal stock, despite his bland appearance and slight stutter, was rising ever higher. And that meant a collision course with new Russian President Vladimir Putin. Putin had made it abundantly clear to this new breed of oligarchs: do business or do politics, but whatever you do, do not do both.

Khodorkovsky, though, did not listen to the clear distinction thrown down by Putin. He used his power and influence at Yukos in lobbying successfully against a new bill to increase oil taxes, in direct contravention of Putin's wishes. It did not help that international player Khodorkovsky was starting to flirt with America. Following the 11 September 2001 attacks in New York, Russian oil gained an instant allure as an alternative to Middle East supplies. It was reported that under the auspices of the Carlyle Group, a Washington-based private equity fund, Khodorkovsky had 'discreet meetings' with George Bush Sr and vice-president Dick

Cheney. Khodorkovsky also started talking about selling off part of Yukos to ExxonMobil, a move that would effectively have allowed Americans to control Russia's natural resources. This too was regarded as politically unacceptable in Russia. He also acquired the rights to publish the prestigious *Moskovskiye Novosti* newspaper, hiring a new, anti-Putin editor.

Things came to a head. The first Kremlin broadside came in July 2003 when Khodorkovsky's business partner Platon Lebedev, also a major shareholder in Yukos, was arrested and accused of having illegally acquired shares in Apatit, a fertilizer company, in 1994. Khodorkovsky was questioned and released two days later. Two weeks later, as the investigation into the Apatit deal widened dramatically, the Russian tax authorities announced that they were planning to audit Yukos's books. The firm's offices were raided and records taken away. Then things got really personal. Khodorkovsky's chartered plane landed at a Novosibirsk airport for refuelling on 25 October 2003, while en route to Irkutsk. At 5 am local time, according to a Yukos statement, it was surrounded by several vehicles with their headlights on. Around 20 black-uniformed agents stormed into the first-class compartment where Khodorkovsky and his entourage of aides and bodyguards were sitting. Brandishing weapons, they apparently shouted, 'FSB! Put your weapons on the ground, don't move or we'll shoot!' Nobody moved.

Khodorkovsky was then flown to Moscow to face various counts of fraud and tax evasion. On 30 October 2003, the Russian authorities froze the 44 per cent stake in Yukos owned by Menatep Bank, and soon after Khodorkovsky resigned as chief executive. But then the fun really started.

In December 2003, Yukos was hit with a US$3.5 billion tax bill for the year 2000. In July the following year it got another bill, this time for US$3.4 billion. Just for good measure, in November 2004 Russian authorities clobbered the firm with a whopping US$10 billion tax bill for alleged unpaid taxes in 2002. In the meantime, on 16 June 2004 Khodorkovsky's Moscow trial began. Prosecutors argued that Khodorkovsky and Lebedev had run an 'organized criminal group'. Khodorkovsky said the charges were 'absurd'.

As the criminal case rumbled on, the prospects for Yukos were looking just as bleak. The firm tried to file for bankruptcy in the United States in an attempt to derail efforts by Russian authorities to sell off the best bits of the business. It did not work. Yuganskneftegaz was eventually sold to the little-known firm Baikalfinansgroup for US$9.35 billion. Then the state-owned oil firm Rosneft bought Baikal, therefore acquiring Yuganskneftegas, and the business was effectively renationalized.

The final verdict on Khodorkovsky was set for 16 May 2005, but it took Judge Irina Kolesnikova an unbelievable 12 days to read it out in full in court. 'Do you understand your sentence?' she asked, finally. 'Yes,' replied Mikhail Khodorkovsky, 'and I also understand that this is a monument to Russian injustice.' Both Lebedev and Khodorkovsky were sentenced to nine years behind bars, almost the maximum penalty possible under Russian law. As if to hammer home the message, Khodorkovsky was dispatched to a Soviet-era prison in the town of Krasnokamensk, in the eastern Siberian province of Chita, near Russia's Chinese border.

It is a very long way indeed from Zhukovka, the elite, gated suburb an hour west of Moscow that Khodorkovsky calls home, although at both he was guarded by men with guns. Inmates at YaG-14/10 can expect to earn 23 roubles a day for prison labour, work that entails sewing protective clothing for the prison system and the police. The average daily temperature in January hovers between -18°C and -33°C. Apparently the average age of the male prisoners is 24, significantly younger than Khodorkovsky, and the most common conviction is for theft.

It is out of sight for the former head of Yukos, but not out of mind. Khodorkovsky continues to plead innocence, and through his supporters and his 'Khodorkovsky & Lebedev Communications Center', he continues to be an irritant to the Russian leadership. On 7 July 2009, he even managed to get an opinion piece published in the *Moscow Times* on 'the prospects for democracy and judicial reform in Russia'. It has to be said that his musings are falling on deaf ears – as of July 2009 Khodorkovsky was up on fresh charges of embezzlement and money laundering, which could lead to a new sentence of up to 27 years.

Opinion in Russia is divided on Khodorkovsky. To many ordinary Russians, the oligarchs are despicable. Khodorkovsky himself admitted to being 'a robber baron', and many poverty-stricken Russians blame their ongoing plight on the likes of the former Yukos head. On the other side of the argument, Putin is blamed by some for carrying out a political vendetta and holding back change in the country.

As with all things in Russia, it is not black and white. Until the main parties publish their warts-and-all autobiographies (which is never), we are unlikely to find out what really happened. 'Putin wants the oligarchs to behave themselves by paying their taxes, to stop stealing assets and behave like normal business people,' says one observer.

As for the languishing Khodorkovsky, it has been an incredible rise and fall, the most dramatic possible. In a long and wide-ranging interview given from prison to the Russian *Esquire* magazine (an interview, incidentally, that resulted in a spell in solitary confinement), it is clear that Khodorkovsky has had plenty of time to think about his predicament. He says at one point:

> God, doom, fate, destiny, nearly everybody believes in something that's higher than us. And indeed it would be strange not to believe, living in a huge unknown world, not really even knowing ourselves; to consider that every-thing around us – is the product of a random confluence of circumstances... If there is no God, and all of our life is but an instant on the way from dust to dust, then what's the point of everything? What's the point of our dreams, our aspirations, our sufferings? What's the point of knowing? What's the point of loving? When it comes right down to it, what's the point of living?

Away from the philosophy, Khodorkovsky seemed to think himself untouchable. There is a fine line between self-belief and delusion, and keeping on the right side of that line is what all great entrepreneurs manage to do. The successful ones convince themselves – and others – that they are better, smarter, more cunning, more visionary or more astute than the people who surround them. It is a vital attribute to have, but it also puts them on a collision cause with self-destruction. Without a brake on that self-belief – or a rational mind to balance the bravado – entrepreneurs like Khodorkovsky are doomed.

That said, it is unlikely that the Khodorkovsky story is over. Until then, it is back to the sewing classes.

SOURCES

BBC, 16 June 2004
BBC, 27 July 2004
BBC, 31 May 2005
BBC, 1 June 2005

BBC, 20 October 2005
Chicago Tribune, 31 May 2005
Daily Telegraph, 3 March 2009
Esquire (Russian edition), 10 October 2008 (see www.esquire.com)
Financial Times, 10 May 2007
Financial Times, 15 May 2008
Forbes, 18 March 2002
Forbes, 1 August 2008
Fortune, 20 September 2004
Kommersant, 22 February 2007
Moscow Times, 7 July 2009
Sunday Times, 13 June 2004
The Times, 21 July 2006
The Times, 17 November 2008
The Times, 4 March 2009
The Times, 27 April 2005
www.khodorkovskycenter.com
www.slate.com, 29 October 2003
www.zabinfo.ruwww.fundinguniverse.com
Also: www.businessweek.com, www.russiatoday.com, www.bloomberg.com, BBC, ITAR-TASS, Associated Press, AFP, Reuters

Chapter Four

Jón Ásgeir Jóhannesson
– Rock Star

The year 2008 was a bad one for Iceland. The country's financial system disintegrated under a banking system that had ballooned to 10 times the size of its economy, and its three major banks, Glitnir, Landsbanki and Kaupthing, all collapsed. By midway through 2008, Iceland's external debt was €50 billion, against a gross domestic product of only €8.5 billion. Icelanders had somehow managed to amass debts of around 850 per cent of their GDP.

The currency, the Icelandic króna, declined more than 35 per cent against the euro from January to September 2008. From trading at 131 to the euro on October 8, it crashed to 340 in a single day. Inflation rocketed to 18.6 per cent – Iceland's economy was in freefall. On 6 October 2008, Iceland's (now ex-) Prime Minister Geir Haarde said there was 'a very real danger... of national bankruptcy'. To compound matters, on 8 October 2008 the British chancellor of the Exchequer, Alistair Darling, announced that the government was taking steps to freeze the assets of the Landsbanki in the United Kingdom under the provisions of the 2001 Anti-terrorism Act.

But it was not just British customers of Landsbanki that were in trouble. Lured by high interest rates, British investors – that's to say individuals, local authorities, companies and charities – had in the region of US$30 billion tied up in all three Icelandic banks and their subsidiaries. And it went further than the United Kingdom. German banks invested US$21 billion, while the Netherlands and Sweden between them invested more than US$700 million. This was not a local problem.

By December 2008, the International Monetary Fund agreed a US$2.1 billion loan for Iceland under its fast-track emergency financing mechanism. A month later, Haarde's government fell apart and for the first time in Iceland, the country voted for a majority left-wing government.

This is Iceland we are talking about – not long ago regarded as the fifth richest nation in the world and ranked as one of the happiest countries in the world! Not any more.

As of 2009 there were more than 30 separate cases being examined by the Icelandic special prosecutor, and international anti-corruption adviser Eva Joly reckons the banking scandal is one of the biggest and most important investigations Europe has ever known. She is already talking in terms of embezzlement, fraud and 'questionable financial practices', and the investigation has only just started.

How on earth did it happen? To understand the economic boom and bust, you need to understand what we are talking about in terms of Iceland. By any stretch of the imagination, it is a weird place. A volcanic rock situated in the north

Atlantic, it is just south of the Arctic circle. It is 287 km from Greenland, 420 km from the Faroe Islands and almost 1,000 km away from mainland Europe in the form of Norway.

The first Norwegians settled on Iceland around 874, but it must have been a godforsaken place. Prone to volcanic eruptions, the only land mammal living on the island when humans first arrived was the Arctic fox. Scientists reckon it came to the island at the end of the ice age, walking over the frozen sea – poor sod. There are no native reptiles or amphibians on the island, and it only boasts 1,300 species of insects, compared with the million or more in the world generally. The point is, the place is isolated.

Iceland was, and remains, good for fishing though, and specifically whale hunting, which can be the only reason anyone would look to live there. Iceland has a long tradition of subsistence whaling, a policy that has continued, with increasing controversy, on and off to this day. The early reliance on whales is reflected in the strange Icelandic language, too. 'Hvalreki' is the word for both 'beached whale' and 'jackpot', which maybe says it all about Iceland.

Size-wise the place is 103,000 square km, not that much smaller than England. Yet it is home to only 300,000 people, whereas around 49 million live in England. In terms of the population, rather than using family names, as is the custom in other mainland European countries, Icelanders use patronymics. Girls add the suffix 'dóttir' (daughter) to the patronymic and boys add 'son'. So Jón Jóhannesson is the son of Johannes. Katrín Karlsdóttir means Katrín, daughter of Karl (the Icelandic telephone directory is listed alphabetically by first name rather than surname). Like many things about Iceland, the names are a little confusing.

And in case you are visiting and are unsure about the Icelandic menu, traditional dishes include cured ram scrota, cured shark, black pudding and, erm, singed sheep heads. So there

47

you have it: small volcanic rock, middle of nowhere, tiny population, unusual names, fishing-based economy, challenging food – oh, and complete and utter financial collapse. So what went wrong and how did it happen so fast?

For centuries, fishing came first in Iceland. Then in 1971, Iceland expanded its zone of exclusive fishing rights to 80 km from the coast, and expanded it further to 320 km in 1975. British fishermen were not very happy about this unilateral move, and the so-called 'cod wars' resulted in mutual net cutting, the ramming of vessels, and ultimately came close to an all-out fight.

But something else also changed. During the 1970s, the Icelandic government introduced fishing quotas. Each fisherman was assigned a quota based on his historical catches. He would then be entitled to a percentage of the catch in any given year. These quotas were worth a great deal, and fishermen could, if they chose not to do the fishing themselves, sell their quota on to someone else. The quotas could even be borrowed against at the banks. And soon, fishing was making a few people very rich indeed.

It was a seminal moment in the financial development of the Iceland economy, and it is familiar territory – financial engineering and clever modelling. Of course not all complicated financial engineering is a bad thing. What is key is that those selling complex financial products understand them – plus they should have a basic entrepreneurial concept of the profit, loss and risk attached to them. History is littered with cases of senior people not really understanding the products and as a result coming unstuck. Iceland was about to come unstuck.

It was this new-found wealth, held by a tiny percentage of the small Icelandic population, that would go on to cause problems. Now gird your loins for an assault of Icelandic names, and try to keep up – it is important.

Three families in particular came to the fore: frozen food entrepreneurs Lýdur Gudmundsson and his brother Ágúst; shipping and brewing moguls Björgólfur Gudmundsson and his son, Thor Björgólfsson; and retail tycoon Johannes Jonsson and his son, the so-called 'pop star' entrepreneur, Jón Ásgeir Jóhannesson.

Lýdur and Ágúst Gudmundsson are co-founders of the Bakkavör food group, which makes ready-meals for the likes of UK retailers Tesco, Asda and Marks & Spencer. They also founded an investment vehicle called Exista, which had a 23 per cent stake in the country's largest bank, Kaupthing. Lýdur was vice-chairman of the bank.

More colourful than those two were Björgólfur Gudmundsson and his son Thor. They were involved in setting up a brewery, called Bravo, in St Petersburg, Russia, eventually selling it to Heineken. They too founded an investment company, with a 32 per cent stake in the country's biggest investment bank, Straumur, and a 45 per cent stake in the second biggest bank, Landsbanki. Björgólfur was chairman of Landsbanki and Thor chairman of Straumur.

And last, but not least, there is Johannes Jonsson and, more to the point, his son Jón Ásgeir Jóhannesson. Jón was born in January 1968, graduated from the Commercial College of Iceland in 1989 and became, aged 21, managing director of his and his father's bargain supermarket business, Bónus. It was the start of a mega rise in the retail sector, which ultimately, under the name of the Baugur Group, took over large chunks of famous UK high street brands and a dizzying number of other interests. Jóhannesson also created an investment vehicle, called Stodir, which took a 32 per cent stake in the country's third largest bank, Glitnir.

So while Iceland is a cold and inhospitable place, its banking and business world was decidedly cosy. Here were these few people with massive stakes in the nation's three banks. And what did these banks do? They lent money to each other. When the dust started to settle following the collapse of the nation's economy, investigators discovered a quite unbelievable state of affairs. Almost half of all the loans made by Icelandic banks were to holding companies, many of which are connected to those same Icelandic banks. These same banks allegedly lent money to employees and associates so they could buy shares in the banks – using the same shares as collateral!

Kaupthing, for example, allowed a Qatari investor to purchase 5 per cent of its shares, but it was later revealed that the Qatari investor bought the stake using a loan from Kaupthing itself. The bank was, in effect, buying its own shares. The notional value of the banks rose.

By far the biggest single loan paid out by Landsbanki UK went to Novator Pharma, a company owned by Björgólfur Thor Björgófsson, the son of Landsbanki's biggest share-holder, and to companies associated with the Baugur Group. In the end, the Baugur Group owed Landsbanki something like ISK58 billion. Ultimately, the entire country's economy was a giant pyramid scheme. And when the credit crunch hit, Iceland was knocked out cold.

Of course during the build-up to the bubble bursting, the entrepreneurial business leaders-cum-bank owners were considered heroes in Iceland. And one man in particular stood out: Jón Ásgeir Jóhannesson. His Reykjavik-based Bónus retail business soon grew to include several outlets in Iceland. In 1992, the owners of Hagkaup, a leading domestic retailer, acquired 50 per cent of the shares in Bónus, and in 1993, Hagkaup and Bónus established a joint purchasing company named Baugur. Baugur, incidentally, means ring of steel. Five years on, with Jóhannesson now Baugur's president and CEO, the business was listed on the Iceland

Stock Exchange. Baugur then embarked on an ambitious acquisitions trail, starting with 50 per cent of the six-strong SMS supermarket chain on the Faroe Islands, 802 km to the southeast of Iceland. And soon he had the United Kingdom in his sights.

It is slightly mystifying how Jóhannesson managed to embark on such an audacious acquisition spree. The odds were rather against this young man from a small rock in the mid-Atlantic turning himself into a global retailing brand, yet he persevered, enthused, cajoled, encouraged and somehow willed it to happen. Perhaps there are similarities with Iceland's Viking past, with mystical powers at work. Or was that black magic simply bravado, over-confidence and showmanship? Whatever it was, it started working.

In 1999 Baugur signed franchise agreements with Sir Philip Green's Arcadia Group, and over the next few years it started snapping up stakes in a host of British retailers, including House of Fraser, Hamleys, Oasis, Karen Millen, Whistles, Coast and the frozen-food chain Iceland. Soon, retail fashion magazine *Drapers Record* had Jóhannesson, with his blond flowing locks and preference for dressing only in black, down as the 'fourth most influential man in the British fashion industry'. That put him behind the likes of Philip Green and Stuart Rose, the director of Marks & Spencer, but above supermodel Kate Moss and designer Karl Lagerfeld.

While Jóhannesson professed to a 'deep dislike of publicity', he enjoyed the high life. Private jets, raucous parties on his private yacht, famous friends and an increasingly global property empire meant that he was rarely away from the gossip columns. In 2007, he married long-time girlfriend Ingibjorg Palmadottir and the pair bought a US$10 million New York apartment. According to the *New York Times*, they liked it so much that they came back a few months later and bought the duplex penthouse above it, with cash, for US$14 million, and hired an architect to design a staircase to combine the places into one 7,000 square foot apartment with 2,000 square feet of terraces.

Meanwhile the Baugur business was split into two main areas. It invested in listed companies with potential, and started getting involved in management takeovers. In May 2004, it acquired a majority stake in the British jewellery chain Goldsmiths. In 2004 the founders of women's fashion chain Karen Millen agreed to sell the business to Baugur Group in a deal worth £120 million. This created a group that included Oasis, Coast, Karen Millen and Whistles, with more than £350 million in sales and 550 stores.

Even these were small fry. In 2004 Jóhannesson was part of a consortium that offered £1 billion for the supermarket group Somerfield, while in 2006 he secured a £351 million deal to buy House of Fraser. He even expressed an interest in buying the Saks department store chain. He was still only in his late 30s.

Ultimately, the Baugur empire had stakes in businesses employing around 65,000 people across 3,800 stores and turning over £10 billion. By any standards, the business was big. By Icelandic standards, it was unprecedented. Yet throughout this period of rapid growth, signs were starting to emerge that all was not as it seemed regarding Jóhannesson and Baugur.

In 2002 Baugur's headquarters were the subject of a police raid, and in July 2005 Jóhannesson and others were charged on 40 counts, including tax and accounting irregular-ities, fraud and embezzlement. Jóhannesson denied the charges, calling them politically motivated, and all but one were dropped. In 2007 he was found guilty (upheld on appeal) on a single charge of a breach of book-keeping rules. Jóhannesson was given a three-month suspended prison sentence, but by relocating the business to the United Kingdom he managed to retain his position on the board of the company.

Yet the writing was on the wall for Baugur and Jóhannesson, and when the global credit crunch hit, the business collapsed, like much of the rest of the Icelandic business so-called miracle. On 4 February 2009, Baugur applied for protection from its creditors and was put into administration.

The inter-bank and inter-business lending and huge debt-fuelled growth strategies could not and would not last. A succession of academics and experts raised concerns – some even directly with the business and political elite – but they were dismissed as either jealous, bitter or somehow racist towards the plucky Icelanders. Allegations of Russian mafia involvement have also been roundly dismissed, and never proved.

Yet in retrospect, the signs were not only there, they were luminous pink, 80 storeys high and flashing 'danger!' It was insanity to believe that this small fishing nation, stuck in the middle of the northern Atlantic, could possibly be up there vying with Wall Street and London's City as a centre of global economic activity. Perhaps it was inevitable.

In a *Lonely Planet* guide book, it says that centuries of isolation and hardship have created a specific national psyche for Iceland. It says that naturally for people living on a remote island in a harsh environment, Icelanders are 'self-reliant individualists who don't like being told what to do'. It cites the example of whaling, saying that while most Icelanders would never eat whale meat, the majority supported hunting – 'a silent sticking-up of two fingers at the disapproving outside world'. The book also wonders, though, whether this confidence is not tinged with inse-curity. 'Icelanders know that it's easy to be a big fish in a small pond, but how might they fare outside their cosy nation?' the book asks. Well, if they did not know before, they know now.

Speaking in March 2009, Jóhannesson admitted that his UK adventure had been a disaster. 'I am still in a state of shock,' he said. 'It all happened so quickly I haven't realized what happened. But it has been a total disaster scenario. I'm sad. I spent 11 years building this up. But I guess this is life. It is what it is.' He continued, 'We definitely had too much on our plate. Not only the retail, but other things that were taking up our time. We will do it differently next time – it will be smaller, more focused.'

Gunnar Sigurdsson, Baugur's UK chief executive, admitted that the group's debt burden had been too heavy. 'Clearly, at the end of the day, the amount of leverage in the business was too much. A once-in-10-years recession we would have survived, but not a once-in-100-years recession. At some point it got a little bit out of control, but we had a great team and we did some really good things along the way.'

Really? While the global recession may have speeded up the collapse, it is stretching credibility to place all the blame at the door of the global economy. The business plan was ill-conceived. They got it wrong. They paid the price.

Jóhannesson, for his part, is talking about dusting himself down and mounting some sort of business comeback, but after such a spectacular fall from grace, and while widely reviled in his now bankrupt homeland, it is unclear what form that will take. Some blame the small population, others talk about the inadequate regulatory oversight. There is talk of the irrational bravado of Icelandic men and the inability to listen to warnings. Ultimately, it was probably a bit of all these things. With investigations ongoing, the truth will out one day. Ultimately, in the case of Jóhannesson, it is about an entrepreneur having a little bit too much self-belief – and far too much debt.

SOURCES

Central Bank of Iceland statistics, www.sedlabanki.is
Daily Telegraph, 19 October 2008
Daily Telegraph, 14 April 2009
Daily Telegraph, 14 June 2009
Drapers Record, December 2004
Economist, 11 December 2008
Government of Iceland, Prime Minister's Office, Address to the Nation by H.E. Geir H Haarde, Prime Minister of Iceland 19 June 208 – http://eng.forsaetisraduneyti.is/news-and-articles/nr/3035
Guardian, 16 June 2005
HM Government, Anti-terrorism, Crime and Security Act 2001: http://www.opsi.gov.uk/Acts/acts2001/ukpga_20010024_en_1
https://www.cia.gov/library/publications/the-world-factbook/geos/ic.html
Ice News, 16 June 2009
Iceland Review, 30 March 2007
International Monetary Fund, Iceland gets help to recover from historic crisis, http://www.imf.org/external/pubs/ft/survey/so/2008/INT111908A.htm
New York Times, 15 February 2009
Observer, 2 September 2007
Sunday Times, 15 March 2009
The Times, 10 December 2007
Vanity Fair, April, 2009
Wall Street Journal, 17 October 2008
www.icelandreview.com
UK Office of Public Sector Information, Landsbanki Freezing Order 2008: http://www.opsi.gov.uk/si/si2008/uksi_20082668_en_1
www.glitnirbank.com
www.kaupthing.com
www.landsbanki.is/english/
Also: BBC News, Press Association, Reuters, *Lonely Planet* (Iceland)

Chapter Five

Reuben Singh
– All That Glitters

The rise and fall of Reuben Singh is a salutary tale for all young and thrusting Asian entrepreneurs in the United Kingdom seeking to make a name for themselves. The rise shows how having youth on your side, being from an ethnic group and being wealthy can rapidly take you to the very heart of government and result in reams of positive press coverage. The fall shows how governments will back anyone they think will make them look good, how fickle a mistress the media can be, and that ultimately all the glitz, glamour and perceived opulence in the world is no replacement for sound business planning.

Singh's parents came to London from Delhi in the 1970s. His father, Sarabjit, was a wealthy wholesaler who imported and sold fashion accessories via a company called Sabco. The family lived in Poynton, an affluent village in Cheshire, and Reuben, the eldest son, was born in 1976. The young Reuben was sent to the William Hulme Grammar School in

Manchester, which has the Latin motto *Fide sed cui vide*, or 'Trust but watch whom you trust'.

Singh was introduced to the family business at a young age, and by the age of 13 he was accompanying his mother on trips to East Asia to buy fabrics. When he was aged 16, his father paid him a regular salary to run the sales department of Sabco. While studying for A-levels, he set up his first business, called Miss Attitude, selling women's clothing, accessories and cosmetics. It was the start of a stellar rise.

Singh opened the first Miss Attitude shop in Manchester's Arndale Centre in 1995, opening another shop four weeks later. By the time he left school, Singh owned nine stores and employed more than 100 people. Ultimately his retail empire would grow to more than 40 shops, and in 1999 Singh sold the business to US financier Gary Klesch's company, Klesch Capital Partners, in a deal worth a reported £22 million.

Still in 1999, he launched AlldayPA in Manchester, 'a 24/7 call answering service'. The business used custom software that enabled a team of personal assistants to handle calls, manage calendars, type letters, and perform other tasks for business owners, all from a central call centre. Singh said he invested 'around £14 million' in the project, adding that he later sold a stake in the business to a consortium of US investors for £10.5 million, valuing AlldayPA at around £116 million. The plan was, he said, to launch the concept in the United States.

It is a common problem: an entrepreneur who has quickly achieved a measure of success becomes impatient to move on to the Next Big Thing. It is hard to say how successful Miss Attitude might have been had Singh stuck with it. We shall never know.

This incredible business success did not go unnoticed by the media, and the praise and accolades started coming.

The *Sunday Times* dubbed him the 'British Bill Gates', and the *Mail on Sunday*'s Rich Report (2001) estimated he was worth more than £80 million. *The Guinness Book of Records* even had Singh down as 'The world's youngest self-made millionaire'. *Fortune* magazine named Singh as Europe's richest entrepreneur under the age of 30, valuing him at more than £95 million, while the *Independent* newspaper put him in its list of people 'ahead of their time'. Singh spoke about his plan to invest some US$50 million in India, and in 2002 he was named Asian Entrepreneur of the Year at a ceremony attended by Prince Charles.

For his part, Singh was not shy about talking up his success. Always one for the soundbite, he came out with various rehashed pearls of wisdom over the years, from 'you'll never throw a six if you don't roll the dice' to 'I don't know anyone who has out-talked me.' That is a strange claim by any standards. He summed up his business philosophy thus: 'I'm not an easy person to do business with. I'll count every penny but I'll never deceive anyone. The golden rule in business is that you never upset your customers.'

Many entrepreneurs enjoy the limelight. It is part of the personality of entrepreneurs to want to show the world what they are made of. Psychologists might argue that this self-justification, or self-glorification, is part of an inner insecurity and inferiority complex. Others would say it is simply part of having a very big ego. For Singh, it was a combination of both.

Courting media attention can undoubtedly help to promote and grow an entrepreneur's business interests. But while journalists sing the praises of up-and-coming entrepreneurs, it is important not to confuse that praise with friendship. The same journalist will be there on the way down, at which point there is little to be gained from complaining about the fairness of it all. Amid the hundreds of magazine and newspaper interviews Singh carried out, he confessed modestly that he did not want to be 'too visible'. So his chosen mode of transport was? That's right, a canary yellow £276,000 Bentley Continental Mulliner. The shy and discerning tycoon's vehicle of choice!

With the media hype machine in full swing, it was not long before Singh came to the attention of UK politicians – always on the lookout for a business success story that might rub off on them. Singh was gold dust. Young, British, Sikh, successful, wealthy – and the political top brass made a beeline for him.

In 1999 the then prime minister Tony Blair set up the Competitiveness Council, a government advisory panel stuffed with the great and the good from UK plc. Alongside the CEOs of British Petroleum, British Telecom, Diageo, PricewaterhouseCoopers, IBM (UK) and GKN, and sat around the table with the then director general of the Confederation of British Industry and head of the Trades Union Congress, was none other than Reuben Singh.

In December that year, then chancellor Gordon Brown launched the National Enterprise Campaign, the latest in a seemingly endless procession of well-meaning initiatives aimed at 'encouraging entrepreneurship' in the United Kingdom. Among those 'business heroes' who signed up for the campaign were Richard Branson, Simon Woodroffe, Alan Sugar, James Dyson, Martha Lane-Fox and, yes, the 23-year-old Reuben Singh. It is hard not to be cynical and believe Singh was there to tick a couple of boxes and make up the numbers. While the other entrepreneurs around the table remain successful business people, it did not quite turn out that way for Singh.

But there was more to come. In May 2000 Singh was appointed to the government's Department of Trade & Industry's now defunct Small Business Council, because 'he showed a very good entrepreneurial spirit and the success of his companies gave us the view that he was a successful businessman'. Singh was described by the Treasury and the British Chambers of Commerce as 'one of a cadre of successful entrepreneurs spearheading a more entrepreneurial culture'. And the ever-bashful Singh told the *Financial Times* in 1999, 'I have instant access to most ministers, most politicians, and most pioneers of industry. I have met Tony Blair many, many, many times and I think he is listening and acting.'

To top even his intimate relationship with Tony Blair, in 2003 Singh was selected by the Davos-based World Economic Forum to take part in its 'Global Leaders for Tomorrow Program'. Singh had made it. Cue the downfall.

The supposed £22 million deal for his Miss Attitude company had always raised eyebrows in the City, and an investigation by the *Manchester Evening News* later discovered that £22 million was something of an over-statement. It was actually bought for £1 – and had debts of more than £1 million. Gary Klesch, who bought the business, was blunt in his appraisal. 'The business was an absolute shambles, and I mean a shambles,' he said. 'Mr Singh is a supreme self-publicist and a very naïve guy, not typical of the type of person we do business with. We have a saying in America – all show, no go – and that sums up the guy completely.'

Klesch wasn't finished there. 'He had a very fancy Mercedes but it turned out it was leased by the company and not owned by him at all. He ran around saying that I paid £55 million for Miss Attitude. Although at the time I knew it was a lie, I couldn't say anything. The deal was subject to a confidentiality clause so I could not say a word. But as he has abused the confidentiality clause, I feel I should tell the truth. If he denies that I bought the company for a pound, let him sue me for libel and a judge can decide who's right. The only reason I bought the company was for its High Street sites.'

At the time, perhaps wisely, Singh declined to comment.

This was not the last of Singh's many business ventures to hit the buffers. His health food business, Robson & Steinberg, went bust owing more than £250,000 after trading for less than a year. One company owed money by Singh said, 'There was always a new excuse. They said that the accounts department was in a different building.' Singh brushed off the difficulties, and supporters said it was part and parcel of being a successful serial entrepreneur: some you win, some you do not. Meanwhile Singh ploughed on. He was soon being referred to as the owner of the Reuben Singh Group of Companies, an organization consisting of 12 trading entities involved in a variety of sectors, from currency trading to property, to retail and construction. Yet newspaper investigations at Companies House found no evidence this corporate entity even existed. Of the seven directorships he was supposed to have held, five of the firms had never filed accounts and the two that had only showed net assets of £1,000 and £100 respectively. Curiouser and curiouser.

It is surprising that the normally sceptical and ever-resourceful British press had allowed such blatant bragging and showmanship to go unchallenged for so long. Then, once the clear fabrications and anomalies came to light, it is equally surprising that no one really pursued them to any great extent. Singh was undaunted by the negative headlines, and they were either dismissed by friends and associates as petty jealousy, or the rather more serious accusation was made that the criticism had racist undertones. Of course it was neither.

But the real trouble had not even started. It did once Singh's parents decided to call in a loan they had made to him. At this point the Bank of Scotland demanded the £1 million-odd it had loaned Singh. He did not have it, but how he came to secure such a big loan from the bank is a tale worth retelling.

It turns out that on one occasion, Singh took the banker handling his account in a chauffeur-driven Mercedes, complete with television in the back, to the Lowry hotel, Manchester, where the banker was treated to the hotel's specially printed 'Reuben Singh menu'. For another meeting Singh had decorated his office with press cuttings about his business successes, including a picture of him meeting best friend Tony Blair, to impress the bank representatives. It worked! A Bank of Scotland employee later admitted he had relied on the press articles in making his decision about Singh.

It was around this point that Singh crossed the blurred line between entrepreneurial showmanship and self-confidence, and misrepresentation. People tend to buy from people or companies that know what they are doing. Entrepreneurs, as a breed, are more aware of this than your average Joe, so naturally they exploit it. But at what point this exploitation goes beyond confidence and boastful showmanship into lying and fraud is open to question.

With the bank now demanding its money back, Singh faced a court appearance, and the full extent – or rather limit – of his business prowess soon came to light. It was not pretty. On 30 October 2007, Manchester County Court judge Michael Kershaw said Singh had deceived the bank to procure the loan. He accepted that Singh had also invented a bank account in Bermuda to help maintain the impression of immense personal wealth.

Details of Singh's financial affairs were laid bare. He owed his father Sarabjit £778,813, and had fallen £12,000 behind in payments for one of his cars. He had also run up debts of around £140,000 on nine credit cards, owed the Inland Revenue £32,500 for a penalty payment and had yet to settle a HM Customs & Excise bill for £60,000. The largest part of Singh's debt was £9 million he owed to a Kuwaiti business, Badr ITK General Trading Company.

In summing up, Judge Kershaw was scathing. 'Mr Singh deliberately and flagrantly deceived the bank about the extent of his personal wealth and ability to honour a guarantee if necessary from cash or realizable securities in the UK,' he said. 'He also liked to keep his own staff in awe of him and in ignorance of the truth of his past and present business activities.' Referring to the former bank employee who had agreed the overdraft with Singh, the judge said the banker was 'to some extent a victim of Mr Singh's personality as well as Mr Singh's lies'.

Singh was declared bankrupt at Manchester County Court with debts estimated at more than £11 million. It was only once the details of the financial arrangements started leaking out that the full picture started to emerge. Accounts from AlldayPA, published in 2003, showed losses of £115,000, debts of £2 million and a £2.6 million payment to Singh that auditors could not account for. On 7 November AlldayPA issued a debenture to Mr and Mrs Singh giving them a claim over an undetermined amount of money from the company. In 2004 Singh, as sole shareholder of ADP Call Centres, decided to increase the capital of the company by issuing more shares. Around 8,000 of these were allocated to Singh's parents, with another 2,000-odd granted to GNDJ Venture Capital Fund of Ontario, Canada, also owned by the Singh family.

Ultimately AlldayPA went into administration, and Singh's parents then bought the company from its receivers. They then installed their own management team at the Salford company, with Reuben reduced to serving as a 'consultant' or 'non-executive chairman'. Speaking at the time, Sarabjit Singh's solicitor said that Reuben 'does not wish to be involved in its day-to-day administration'. He was well and truly on the naughty step.

It is questionable to what extent Singh really was an entrepreneur. For one, he does not appear to have ever made any money. And he seems to have preferred to hang on to the coat tails of his family. Yet they could not save him. The downfall was complete. The press, once so full of praise, were vitriolic. They said Singh was 'exposed as a charlatan' and that he 'proved himself to be a brilliant self-publicist'. 'Singh has managed to convince the business establishment, the Blair administration and the world's financial press into believing he is a multi-millionaire,' exclaimed the *Mail on Sunday* newspaper. 'In reality, he is little more than a fantasist.'

There is a common complaint in the United Kingdom that the British media 'build people up and knock them down'. It is something people would recognize in many countries. But it is an over-simplification, and glosses over the fact that the vast majority of the people who receive positive press coverage work extremely hard to get it, employing batteries of eager public relations executives to generate the headlines and features.

The press do not seek out random business people and build them up, yet entrepreneurs like Singh, caught out and found out, do not appear to appreciate that the media are a double-edged sword. They are looking for stories, headlines and angles. If someone new comes along, someone young, Sikh, successful, wealthy, it is little wonder the press trip over themselves to put that face on their covers. But it comes at a cost. As soon as business people court the media, they need to watch out. And if they're up to no good, they should not court it at all.

SOURCES

Daily Telegraph, 2 May 2007

Department for Culture, Media and Sport (DCMS) The pale yellow amoeba: a peer review, 2000 http://www.culture.gov.uk/reference_library/publications/4685.aspx

Department of Trade and Industry (DTI) *Our Competitive Future, UK Competitiveness Indicators 1999*

HM Treasury, www.hm-treasury.gov.uk/press_210_99.htm, 9 December 1999

http://www.sathnam.com/Features/71/reuben-singh

Independent, 6 June 2006

Independent, 1 October 2007

Mail on Sunday, 15 December 2002

Mail on Sunday, 21 March 2004

Management Today, 1 June 2001

Manchester Evening News, 13 December 2002

Manchester Evening News, 13 January 2003

Manchester Evening News, 12 March 2004

Manchester Evening News, 23 September 2005

Manchester Evening News, 30 October 2007

Real Business magazine, 2001

Sunday Times, 12 October 2003

Times Online, 27 October 2002

World Economic Forum 'Global Leaders for Tomorrow Program 2003'

www.ameinfo.com/60759.html, 23 May 2005

Other sources: *Real Business* magazine, alldaypa.com, www.genesis-initiative.org, http://www.sikhfoundation.org/comprof0802.asp

Chapter Six

Tim Power
– More Than He Could Chew

The Brenninkmeyers are the Dutch family dynasty behind the C&A clothing empire. Today, a Swiss-based holding company called the Cofra Group controls the business, which traces its history back to 1841, although its supervisory board still contains four of the Brenninkmeyer family. The business runs major retail operations throughout the world – in the United States, Asia and Europe – but it has also moved into financial services, real estate, private equity, and more recently runs a renewable energy portfolio. The close-knit family's combined personal wealth is estimated at something like £2.5 billion.

Into this family (motto: 'Unity makes strength'), in 1988, married Tim Power. And his life would change forever.

It must have seemed like an extraordinary result for Power, going overnight from a lowly barman to someone for whom money would seemingly never be a problem again. By marrying Chantal Brenninkmeyer, heiress to the dynasty, Power would be set for life. Only it did not turn out that way.

Timothy Power was born in the mid-1960s. His father had a successful career as a civil engineer, which included building the mass transit system in Hong Kong, but son Tim was not destined to follow in his footsteps. With poor A level grades, Power junior opted for catering college before embarking on a career in the hospitality trade. But what a career!

Power started out as a barman in a King's Road bar called Henry J Beans. An 'American-style bar and grill', it was to set the pattern for Power's working life. He learned the ropes and moved to Paris where he became a manager of the Chicago Pizza Pie Factory, a restaurant just off the Champs-Élysées. One review describes it thus: 'The sounds of American rock music fills the Americana-laden walls of this country and western-style bar. And remember, one pizza is generally enough for two people.'

But it was not enough for the 6ft 7in Power. He harboured ambitions to be 'bigger' than British restaurant guru Terence Conran, and had heady plans of world domination. And while Power's father was wealthy, his marriage to Brenninkmeyer put him in a different league.

But it was not all good. Within a year, Power claims he was unhappy. 'Her family were very strange and controlling,' he told an interviewer later. 'Everything was done for you. If you wanted to book a flight, if you wanted a chauffeur, you spoke to someone. It was horrifying for someone who was only 23.' As a result of his unhappiness with his new-found wealth and freedom, Power threw himself into his work, and by his own admission, was 'extremely' badly behaved.

Power then got a job at yet another US-themed chain of restaurants, this time owned by flamboyant Texan millionaire Charles Burnett III. Burnett was, and remains, something of a character, and in 1999 this nephew of Lord Montagu of Beaulieu was included in the *Guinness Book of World Records* for an offshore water speed record of 137 mph. Power worked for his restaurant business and also ran the tycoon's powerboat team. 'We would travel all over the world in private jets,' noted Power. 'We would go to New Orleans for the day. We'd go to New York for the weekend. There were a couple of occasions when I woke up in bed and thought: "Who's this? Where am I? And why is my car parked at a funny angle in the street below?"'

Power's life was starting to spin out of control. His first business venture was to set up a bar/club in Chelsea's King's Road called Embargo. It bombed. Despite money being no barrier and his experience in the trade, the bar lost £80,000 in five months and closed.

It is difficult to avoid alcohol if you work in the hospitality trade, and Power could not say no. By 1995, aware of the impact his drinking was having on his marriage to Chantal, and on his two daughters, Chelsea and Savannah, he signed up to Alcoholics Anonymous.

A year later, in 1996, came Power's big break when he joined the Belgo restaurant chain as operations manager. Belgo specializes in Belgian cooking and Belgian beer – 'moules and frites' – and it is also noted for its waiting staff who dress as monks. Founded in 1992 by French-Canadian Denis Blais and Anglo-Belgian Andre Plisnier, the business was bought in 1996 by serial entrepreneur Luke Johnson (he sold his stake in 2005, and today the business is run by Tragus Ltd). The business started as a small north London affair, but soon opened branches in central London and throughout the United Kingdom. Business was good.

Power was in his element and put his years of experience into practice. He spoke in lofty tones about his 'one-man crusade against mediocrity', and he certainly worked long, 16-hour days. Yet while he was sometimes described as 'an excellent motivator', his methods were also said to be 'brutal'. A notorious disciplinarian, he would bawl people out for trivial matters. 'I hate things that are done badly,' he told the *London Evening Standard* in 1998. 'I am a very harsh critic of everyone and everything – myself more than anyone else.'

He also, apparently, prided himself on not speaking to anyone on the phone for longer than 60 seconds. 'Phone calls are generally unproductive unless they are telling you something,' he said. 'If you get 100 phone calls in a day and you keep them to a minute instead of two, that's another eight hours a week you can devote to something more useful.'

The man was driven. He played hard too. Yet he was also turning the Belgo business around. He fired most of the management team and a third of the staff, but in a year, the company's profits almost doubled. Power was given a shareholding and made a director. He was finally coming out from Chantal's shadow.

Then, in December 1997, Belgo was involved in a 'reverse takeover' by cash shell Lonsdale Holdings in a deal worth £9.8 million. It then took over three fashionable restaurants, Daphne's (a favourite of Princess Diana's), The Collection and Pasha, in a £10 million deal. A few months later, Belgo paid £15 million for three more of London's most prestigious restaurants – the Ivy (frequented by the likes of David and Victoria Beckham), Le Caprice and J Sheekey. As operations manager, Power made £500,000 from the takeover, and promptly bought himself a Ferrari. It is said that at one point he was updating his car every three or four weeks. Why not?!

It was a heady period in Britain, and in London in particular. City bonuses were big, the dotcom boom was making a few people very rich indeed, and the gossip columns were full of salacious tales of debauchery, drink and drugs among the capital's elite. Even the new British government, headed by Tony Blair, was getting in on the act, hosting lavish receptions for the country's hip and trendy fashion-setters. Cool Britannia was the call to arms, and the likes of Tim Power revelled in it.

In some ways, Power was the epitome of the new-look Britain – a modest background but now taking on the world. And on the face of it, there is absolutely nothing wrong with that. Britain needs more people to have this mindset. Power had made it. Operations director at a firm running some of London's and the world's finest restaurants, hobnobbing with the likes of Elton John and George Michael, Power was in his element.

But his professional success came at a heavy price in his personal life. In 1998 he discovered that his wife was having an affair, with a City trader called Tim Lowe. Power apparently managed to track down Lowe's number and threatened to kill him. It was clear Power's relationship with Chantal was over. The two divorced and she won custody of the two children. It was, Power says, a bitter blow.

But worse was to come. Perhaps, in part, slightly antagonized by Power's death threat, Lowe proceeded to contact the London Stock Exchange, reporting Power for insider trading. It was a serious allegation, and one that was to have major ramifications for him.

In the meantime, Power quit Belgo. Although there was no suggestion his departure was linked with the police probe, his bosses now claim he 'jumped before he was pushed'. At the time, the arrangement was dressed up as an amicable split. Later that year, the hapless Power reportedly 'lost a fortune on the stockmarket'.

But he was not finished in the bar/club game. In 2000, he set up another bar venture in Leeds – somewhat improbably with Goldie, the British musician-cum-DJ, and former football hardman-turned-actor Vinne Jones. Power also set up various other businesses, called Linpower, Powerlin and Forward Choice plc.

It is actually quite typical for entrepreneurs on the up to associate themselves with 'C' and 'D' list celebrities. Money brings them opportunities, and Power, managing a series of high-profile London restaurants, would have come into contact with a whole host of minor celebs.

It was around this time that Power's old boss Charles Burnett got in touch – perhaps to talk about old times, maybe to discuss an upcoming business project. Unbeknown to Power, and at the direction of the Department of Trade and Industry (DTI), Burnett was packing a hidden microphone in an attempt to extract a confession about the insider trading. The walls were closing in. Yet before the DTI case came to court, Power was up on other charges relating to his beloved Ferrari.

In August 1999, a police officer in Aberarth, west Wales, spotted a tax disc on the Ferrari 355 which actually belonged to a Mercedes owned by a Bristol car rental firm. Later police checks on the Ferrari found it to have a different tax disc, this time from a blue BMW convertible owned by Paul Smith Ltd in Nottingham. In December 1999, the car once again came to the attention of the police when it was found parked on double yellow lines in Trafalgar Square, London, allegedly with no tax disc at all.

Of all places to leave a car on a double yellow line in London, about the least sensible is Trafalgar Square. It is one of the busiest thoroughfares in London, teeming with tourists, buses, taxis, cars and police officers offering directions, and most normal people would not dream of parking a car there. And if they did they could be fairly confident that it would not be there for long. It is an insight into the way Power's mind was working at the time: it was as if normal rules did not apply.

On each of the three occasions the police noticed his car, it was carrying the 'P9WER' number plate which had applied to a Porsche 911 owned by Power, but which had lapsed in March 1999. Whatever was going on, the courts wanted to hear about it, and Power was set a hearing date at Blackfriars Crown Court for October. He did not show up. An arrest warrant was duly issued, and Power was eventually hauled before the court on five counts of fraudulently using a registration plate and three counts of fraudulently using a vehicle licence on his £70,000 car.

Despite his interest in cars, Power told the court he knew nothing about the purchasing of tax discs. 'I was very, very spoilt and cosseted as far as that goes,' he said. 'When I was married to my wife everything was taken care of by the bank she owned.' He also claimed that he normally 'relied on chauffeurs' to sort out matters such as road tax. Unimpressed, the judge sentenced Power to 120 hours community service.

Bizarrely, and somewhat ironically, in 2001 Power cropped up in the news, again to do with cars – this time as part of a team planning to stage a 'Gumball rally' illegal car race across the United States. The plan was to run the thing with an entrepreneur called Sunny Dhown, who had a conviction for drink-driving.

It was not the end of Power's legal woes, either. In February 2002, he was sentenced to two years at Leeds Crown Court for theft and obtaining money transfers by deception.

But the worst was yet to come for Power – and in quite dramatic style.

In April 2008, Power travelled into the United Kingdom on a United Airlines flight to watch Chelsea play football, apparently at the invitation of then head coach Avram Grant. But before Power managed to get out of his first-class seat, four armed police officers boarded the plane and arrested him on charges of insider trading. Power would not be watching the football that day – he would be spending it in a police cell. And two days later, after being denied bail, he was moved to Wandsworth Prison in south London for a five-month pre-trial wait, alongside some of Britain's most dangerous inmates.

HM Prison Wandsworth is a category B/C men's prison and one of the toughest in the United Kingdom. It is the place where William Joyce (Lord Haw-Haw) was executed, and has also been home to hardened criminals such as 1960s gang leader Ronnie Kray, 'Great train robber' Ronnie Biggs and notorious inmate Charles Bronson. In December 1999, an inspection report stated that there was 'a pervasive culture of fear' at the jail, and that staff were 'callous and uncaring' and guilty of intimidation, racism and sexism.

It would be tough work for the 6ft 7in Power to keep his head down. 'One of my cell mates was a Jamaican yardie who had killed a policeman,' he later recalled. 'He had several bullet wounds and stab wounds. There were several fights, normally in the dinner queue, and I once saw a guy trying to cut another guy's head off. I decided the best way to protect myself was to say as little as possible and stay in my cell.'

The maximum jail sentence for insider dealing is seven years. So Power had plenty to think about. When his case finally came to trial, it was the United Kingdom's first insider dealing trial for four years. Southwark Crown Court heard that Euan Carlisle, a former company director, had used confidential information passed to him by a senior employee of Belgo – that is, Power – to buy shares ahead of two crucial company announcements. 'The information related to two very important events in the life of Belgo,' said Sarah Whitehouse, for the prosecution. 'It was information which was bound, when it became public, to affect the share price.' The insider dealing occurred ahead of the £10 million reverse takeover of Belgo in December 1997 and the announcement of the restaurant acquisitions the following May.

On both occasions, said Whitehouse 'the share price went up [after it became public knowledge] and he sold all the shares, making a handsome profit. This sort of conduct, known as insider dealing, is a criminal offence. The passing on of confidential information by those inside a company, and the dealing in shares on the strength of that information, is a fraud. It is cheating.' Whitehouse added that the two men had numerous phone calls leading up to the public pronouncements and dismissed talk that this was down to pure chance.

The most salacious aspect of the case came to light during pre-trial legal argument. Lawyer Simon Williams, at the time an investigator for the DTI, was asked how Power's name first emerged during investigations into Belgo and Lonsdale share dealings. 'From recollection,' he said, 'I think there was someone called Chantal Brenninkmeyer who had been married to Mr Power and had some association… a love triangle, or whatever you want to call it.' The headline writers were delighted.

After the Crown was given permission to include the damning audio transcripts of Power's bugged phone calls in its case, he changed his plea from not guilty to guilty, admitting two counts of insider trading between 15 October

1997 and 20 May the following year. In mitigation, Power's lawyer Jonathan Goldring said his client 'socialized in very wealthy circles but was never himself in the financial Ivy League. Now he is broken, he is single, he is unemployable and he is a convicted criminal.' He also read a statement from Power, who tried to blame his wife's infidelity for his own law-breaking. The judge was having none of it.

Passing sentence, Judge James Wadsworth QC said:

> The offences to which you pleaded guilty are serious because they are a grave breach of trust by someone at the centre of a company which is going to cause sensitive movement on the Stock Exchange and upon which other people are relying for honesty and transparency. You went deliberately behind it.

The judge continued, 'Matters were made worse because you did it on two separate occasions in respect of two quite separate items of knowledge.'

The facts that the offence took place 12 years previously, and that Power had already served 163 days in prison, led the judge to sentence him to 18 months suspended for two years. The DTI, by now the Department for Business Enterprise and Regulatory Reform, said it hoped the case would 'provide some deterrent'. After the case, Power claimed he only changed his plea to get a lighter sentence. He said he had plans to return to Italy, where he lives with his girlfriend.

Despite all that happened to him, Power remains remarkably unrepentant. 'I haven't had a fall from grace,' he told one newspaper following the conviction. 'I'm the luckiest man alive. I've learnt what not to do and who not to be around and that's a valuable lesson. I've never been happier.' Power's psychiatrist deserves a pay rise.

SOURCES

Companies House, www.companieshouse.gov.uk
Daily Telegraph, 26 February 2009
Daily Telegraph, 3 March 2009
Daily Telegraph, 7 March 2009
Department for Business, Innovation and Skills, www.berr.gov.uk
Financial Services Authority, www.fsa.gov.uk
Guardian, 25 February 2009
Herbert Smith, Financial regulation briefing, May 2009
Independent, 28 July 2000
Independent, 9 February 2001
Independent, 21 March 2001
London Evening Standard, 8 February 2001
London Evening Standard, 13 May 2002
London Evening Standard, 2 March 2009
Reuters, 2 March 2009
Sunday Times, 12 December 2001
The Times, 23 February 2009
The Times, 26 February 2009
www.belgo-restaurants.com
www.caprice-holdings.co.uk
www.channel4.com, 8 July 2009
www.cofraholding.com
www.hmprisonservice.gov.uk
www.securitiesdocket.com/2009/02/15
www.steamcar.co.uk
www.tragusholdings.com

Chapter Seven

Dick Fuld
– King Kong

The extraordinary collapse of 158-year-old investment bank Lehman Brothers shocked the financial world. Its dramatic demise hastened panic on international markets and no doubt contributed towards what would become known as the global credit crunch of 2008. Its route was sub-prime mortgage lending, and at the head of Lehman Brothers was Dick Fuld.

Richard Fuld, or Dick as he preferred to be known, was born in New York in 1946. He graduated from the University of Colorado in 1969. He had plans of becoming a test pilot or an aeronautical engineer, but this ambition was not helped by a fight with a commanding officer, and it was not to be. It was not for nothing that Fuld would later gain the nickname 'the gorilla'.

Instead, Fuld got a job at Lehman Brothers. He never left. Fuld started out as a commercial paper trader, but he took night classes at New York University's Stern School of Business, and in 1973 attained an MBA. He was destined for greater things.

Founded in 1850 in Montgomery, Alabama, Lehman Brothers started out as a cotton trading business. In the beginning, it was just German-Jewish immigrant brothers Emanuel, Mayer and Herbert (or Henry) Lehman. The brothers established the New York Cotton Exchange, and before long Lehman Brothers was financing the growth of railroads as Americans pushed west, and funded legendary American businesses such as Sears, Roebuck and Woolworth's. The Lehman family became part of the New York aristocracy, with Herbert becoming the 45th governor of New York and later a US senator. Herbert's cousin Robert ran the firm from 1925 until his death in 1969 – the year Fuld started.

Lehman Brothers' more recent history is slightly more convoluted. In 1977 it merged with Kuhn, Loeb & Co to form Lehman Brothers, Kuhn, Loeb Inc, becoming the country's fourth-largest investment bank. But infighting was rife and the company suffered. The business was sold to Shearson, an American Express-backed company, in 1984, for US$360 million. The situation did not last, though, with Lehman Brothers being spun out of American Express in 1994. The business went public, trading as Lehman Brothers Holdings. At its helm was the head of the fixed income division, Dick Fuld. The year before Fuld took over, Lehman Brothers made a loss of US$102 million. By 1994 it had 9,000 employees and US$75 million in earnings.

It is the sort of widely acclaimed track record of success that makes people believe they can do no wrong. The more it continues, the more unquestioning people become of the leader, whose position becomes impregnable. Other executives, transfixed by the leader, become more concerned about details than the bigger picture. The CEO's personal whims start to take on increased importance, and people take their eyes off the ball.

Between 1994 and 2007, Lehman Brothers' market capitalization grew from US$2 billion to US$45 billion. Its share price went from US$5 to US$86, creating an average annual return for shareholders of 24.6 per cent. It grew to more than 28,000 employees, with more than 60 offices in over 28 countries. The one man behind this incredible growth was Dick Fuld. One reason for it was that by 2006, Lehman Brothers was the number one underwriter of securities backed by sub-prime mortgages. This sub-prime lending was the riskiest of the lot.

Between the years 1993 and 2007, Fuld reportedly received nearly half a billion dollars in total compensation. In 2007 alone, he earned a total of US$22 million, including a base salary of US$750,000, a cash bonus of US$4,250,000, and stock grants of US$16 million. Fuld was chairman of the board of directors and CEO. He was king.

In addition to his roles within Lehman Brothers, Fuld was in demand elsewhere. He served on the board of directors of the Federal Reserve Bank of New York, and was a member of the International Business Council of the World Economic Forum and the Business Council. He served on the Board of Trustees of Middlebury College and New York-Presbyterian Hospital. And in addition to all this, he was on the board of directors of the Robin Hood Foundation, 'a charitable organization which attempts to alleviate problems caused by poverty in New York City'. Fellow directors included Harvey Weinstein, Marie-Josee Kravis, Lloyd Blankfein of Goldman Sachs and actress Gwyneth Paltrow.

This is not merely a veneer of respectability, it is part of the driver and motivation for success. As Tom Wolfe illustrates in *The Bonfire of the Vanities*, this social and community recognition is of paramount importance to the egotistical entrepreneur – although never more important than the money itself. Plus, let us not forget the impact of Fuld's good work.

The Lehman Brothers staff were not doing too badly either. The staff received a disproportionately high percentage of their pay in Lehman stock and options. When the firm went public, employees owned 4 per cent of the firm, worth US$60 million. By 2006, they owned around 30 per cent, equivalent to US$11 billion, at least on paper. That meant a lot of people suffered financial and emotional pain when things went wrong.

The media hype was that Lehman was one big happy family, with all staff sharing in the success of the others. Yet in the hard-nosed world of investment banking this is rarely the case, and it was not the case with Lehman Brothers. In the quest for greater profits, more risks were taken and little heed was given to those brave enough to advise caution. In fact caution was not a word often heard at Lehman Brothers. The unbridled greed would lead to dramatic consequences.

It is odd that film director Oliver Stone, in his film *Wall Street*, and the likes of Tom Wolfe in his books, were so much quicker to recognize the problems associated with this behaviour than senior economists and government regulators. The bankers themselves were in too deep, oblivious, selfish and arrogant. The City of London and Wall Street characterized themselves as the engines of growth – stressing that the rest of the population should be thankful, not questioning. While things were good, few did question. While governments were on the receiving end of tax payments (at least, those taxes the banks paid, since they worked hard to avoid paying as much as possible), it is easy to see why few questions were being asked.

By 2007, Lehman Brothers was the largest trader of stocks on the London Stock Exchange and had a role in a fifth of all corporate takeovers. In 2003, it purchased asset management business Neuberger Berman for US$3 billion. The next year, it bought California-based BNC Mortgage, a company that specialized in making sub-prime loans. Lehman also bought Aurora Loan Services, another lender that specialized in loans made to borrowers without full documentation. In the first half of 2007, Aurora was originating more than US$3 billion a month of such loans.

So why was Lehman buying these firms? Lehman's trick was to repackage mortgage loans into bonds. Lehman reported record earnings in 2005, 2006 and 2007. Lehman's shareholders reaped a 17-fold increase from 1994 to its peak in February 2007. But the whole lot was built on quicksand: dodgy mortgages that could never and would never be repaid.

Before the credit crunch occurred, though, Lehman Brothers bore witness to an altogether more devastating event in the form of the 9/11 attacks on New York. While it did not suffer as badly as bond trading firm Cantor Fitzgerald, with its shocking 658 fatalities, the Lehman Brother offices were directly adjacent to the World Trade Center towers, with all the horrors that must have presented. Lehman's headquarters suffered massive damage and its lobby was used as a morgue. For Lehman Brothers, though, work went on, and by Wednesday 12 September, the firm was open for business. The company even managed to post near-record results for the month.

But Lehman Brothers' ability to survive what was thrown at it, an admirable quality in terrible times, would not last much longer, and seven years later it would be gone. A company that as of February 2008 was worth something like US$42 billion, with total assets of US$639 billion, would soon be worth nothing. Fuld tried to hold off the inevitable with bold statements of intent and typically confrontational rebuttals to questioning journalists, but it was hopeless.

On 15 September 2008, Lehman Brothers Holdings filed for Chapter 11 bankruptcy protection. Its bankruptcy filing listed debts of US$613 billion, and named banks from Tokyo, Hong Kong, New York, Singapore, Taipei and elsewhere as unsecured creditors owed hundreds of millions of dollars.

On 6 October 2008, Fuld was requested to testify before the US House Committee on Oversight and Government Reform on Capitol Hill. It wanted to know what went wrong. Fuld was unapologetic. While admitting he felt 'horrible about what happened', he set about apportioning blame. 'Ultimately what happened to Lehman Brothers was caused by a lack of confidence,' he said. 'The second issue I want to discuss is naked short selling, which I believe contributed to both the collapse of Bear Stearns and Lehman Brothers.... The final issue I will address is the changed landscape of our financial system and regulatory regime'. He added, 'Not that anyone on this committee cares about this but I wake up every single night wondering what I could have done differently'. That said, Fuld reckoned his decisions were 'prudent and appropriate' given the information he had at the time. In other words, it was not his fault.

To many on Wall Street, not least because of his long tenure at the company, Fuld was Lehman Brothers personified. Without him, it would not have become a global giant, they said. Admirers described him as 'an unbelievable competitor'. While some media puff pieces claimed he was 'obstinate, determined and accountable', others called him 'aggressive, confrontational, blunt'.

While the case against Dick Fuld is clear, of course he was not the only person at fault. There were other factors that came into play above and beyond the toxic assets. It is worth mentioning Hank Paulson, the 74th US Treasury

Secretary and a long-time adversary of Fuld. The two were competitors for more than 20 years while Paulson was a managing partner at Goldman Sachs. Could Paulson, as Treasury Secretary, have stepped in to save Lehman Brothers and Fuld? For whatever reasons, he chose not to. Others implicated in the fall of Lehman Brothers include the 75th US Treasury Secretary Timothy Geithner. The former president of the Federal Reserve Bank of New York, Geithner was initially vociferous in supporting the government's refusal to bail out the firm, according to people involved in various meetings at the time.

Since Geithner became the Treasury Secretary, the Obama administration has attempted to put some distance between him and Paulson, saying that Geithner did indeed press to save the firm from bankruptcy, but that he was a 'lone voice on the subject' and was 'overruled' by Paulson and Ben Bernanke, the Federal Reserve chairman, on this issue. Andrew Ross Sorkin, writing in the *New York Times* on 25 November 2008, said, 'Many executives suggest it may be a bit of revisionist history.'

In Ken Auletta's 1987 book *Greed and Glory on Wall Street*, Dick Fuld is described as 'someone who spent so much time in front of his green screen or making rat-tat-tat decisions that he was no longer human'. Fuld was big on references to warfare, seeing Lehman Brothers somehow as 'being at war' with the competition. 'Every day is a battle,' he said, adding that staff should always 'think about the firm, do the right thing, protect your client, protect the firm, be in it, be a good team member'.

As if to back this up, Fuld ended the practice of casual dress at Lehman Brothers. 'If you dress sloppy, you think sloppy,' he said, and he was particularly pleased one time when a journalist remarked that he could spot Lehman Brothers employees by their attire. The women dressed conservatively and the men almost exclusively in white or blue shirts and ties. The employees were the troops, in their uniforms, and Fuld was the leader.

The most fascinating insight into Fuld comes from Andrew Gowers, a former editor of the London *Financial Times*, who in June 2006 joined Lehman Brothers in London as head of corporate communications. In a remarkable account of the final days of Lehman Brothers, published in the *Sunday Times* on 14 December 2008, Gowers cast a light on the culture of Lehman Brothers and the psyche of its boss. 'To say he was surrounded with a cult of personality would be an understatement,' said Gowers. He called Fuld 'almost unbearably intense', and said he inspired great loyalty and fear. 'Those closest to him slaved like courtiers to a medieval monarch,' Gowers said, 'second-guessing his moods and predilections, fretting over minute details of his schedule down to the flower arrangements and insulating him from trouble – from almost anything he might not want to hear.' How does a CEO run a business only hearing the good news?

This culture would be Fuld's undoing. It meant that no one would, or could, challenge him. And while this might not have mattered in the 55 quarters of unbroken profit, Gowers said it bred 'a fatal complacency'.

Fuld was aware that trouble was brewing back in January 2007. During a press briefing in the Swiss mountain resort of Davos during the World Economic Forum, he told assembled newspaper editors 'this could be the year when the markets crack'. If only he had taken his own advice. He mentioned potential trouble in the US housing market, the problem of the excesses of leveraged finance and the danger of spiralling oil prices – and the explosive combination of all three. He told the editors that as a result of these potential problems, Lehman Brothers had become more cautious and 'taken a bit of money off the table'. But Gowers says this talk was completely at odds with the reality of how Lehman Brothers was being run. 'In truth Fuld had become insulated from the day-to-day realities of the firm and had increasingly delegated operational authority to his number two, a long-standing associate named Joe Gregory,' he said.

The problem with this strategy, said Gowers, was that Gregory was not a detail man or a risk manager. In fact, he added, Gregory was actively urging divisional managers to place even more aggressive bets in surging asset markets such as the mortgage business and commercial real estate. In one Lehman-led deal in June 2007, it bid US$15 billion for America's biggest apartment company – a deal signed off by the entire executive committee and subsequently described as 'the worst investment Lehman ever made'.

Yet again, we see a failing firm making a last-gasp deal. This US$15 billion failure was to be the worst deal ever – but is that what they really wanted? No, they simply had no other options – the *Titanic* was heading for the iceberg, so they pushed up the engines to full throttle.

Gowers characterized the corporate governance structure as:

> almost pre-programmed to fail: an overmighty CEO, a top lieutenant eager to please and hungry for risk, an executive team not noted for healthy debate and a power struggle between two key players. Furthermore, the board of directors was packed with non-executives of a certain age and woefully lacking in banking expertise.

It was to prove a toxic combination. The man in the middle was Dick Fuld.

SOURCES

Anderson, Jenny (2007) The survivor, *New York Times*, 28 October [online]http://www.nytimes.com/2007/10/28/business/28fuld.html?pagewanted=1 (accessed 11 February 2010)

Auletta, K (1987) *Greed and Glory on Wall Street: The fall of the house of Lehman*, Penguin, London

Bawden, Tom (2008) Bruiser of Wall St Dick Fuld looked after his people, but didn't know when to quit, *The Times*, 16 September [online] http://business.timesonline.co.uk/tol/business/industry_sectors/banking_and_finance/article4761890.ece (accessed 15 February 2010)

Clark, Andrew (2008) You might think Lehman boss Fuld would be chastened, *Guardian*, 8 October [online] http://www.guardian.co.uk/business/2008/oct/08/lehman-brothers.banking1 (accessed 11 February 2010)

English, Simon (2008) Profile: Lehman Bros boss Richard Fuld, *Evening Standard* (London), 19 March

Equilar (nd) Richard S. Fuld Jr [online] http://www.equilar.com/CEO_Compensation/LEHMAN_BROTHERS_HOLDINGS_INC_Richard_S._Fuld_Jr.php (accessed 11 February 2010)

Gowers, Andrew (2008) Dick Fuld, the man who brought the world to its knees, *Sunday Times*, 14 December 2008 [online] http://business.timesonline.co.uk/tol/business/industry_sectors/banking_and_finance/article5336179.ece (accessed 11 February 2010)

Reuters.com (2009) Sold his house for $100, 25 January [online] http://www.reuters.com/article/idUSTRE50P04A20090126 (accessed 11 February 2010)

Robison, Peter and Onaran, Yalman (2008) Fuld's subprime bets fueled profit, undermined Lehman, Bloomberg, 15 September [online] http://www.bloomberg.com/apps/news?pid=20601170&refer=home&sid=aiETiKXNbDVE (accessed 15 February 2010)

Serwer, Andy (2006) The improbable power broker: how Dick Fuld transformed Lehman from Wall Street also-ran to super-hot machine, *Fortune*, 13 April

Story, Louise (2008) At Lehman, chief exudes confidence, *New York Times*, 17 June

TheStreet.com (nd)

Time (nd) 25 people to blame for the financial crisis [online] http://www.time.com/time/specials/packages/article/0,28804,1877351_1877350_1877326,00.html (accessed 15 February 2010)

Wall Street Journal, 15 September 2008

wikipedia (nd) Robin Hood Foundation [online] en.wikipedia.org/wiki/Robin_Hood_Foundation (accessed 11 February 2010)

Wikipedia (nd) Richard S. Fuld, Jr

Financial Times, 22 December 2008

Forbes.com, 16 April 2008

www.bbc.co.uk

www.robinhood.org

Chapter Eight

Guy Naggar and Peter Klimt
– The Art of Money

Sleep Dealer was a debut film by director Alex Rivera. The blurb runs, 'Set in a near-future, militarized world marked by closed borders, virtual labor and a global digital network that joins minds and experiences, three strangers risk their lives to connect with each other and break the barriers of technology.' The 2008 film, set in the state of Oaxaca and the city of Tijuana, Mexico, received mixed reviews.

Time Out Chicago called it 'impressive but unsatisfying', the *San Francisco Chronicle* said it was 'flawed, but still vibrant and inventive', while the *New York Press* reported the film as 'a well-meaning failure'. Film reviewing website nerve.com summed it up thus: 'The film culminates in an unconvincing finale whose hopefulness seems not only fanciful but, when viewed on the story's own terms, woefully short-sighted.'

The reviews could well be used to sum up the business careers of the film's two executive producers: Guy Naggar and Peter Klimt, otherwise known as the men behind collapsed property and financial empire Dawnay, Day. That one of the biggest complaints about the film was that it 'obviously suffered budgetary constraints' may come as a surprise as the pair were loaded. But then money cannot buy success.

More to the point, though, what on earth were Naggar and Klimt doing as executive producers on a small independent US film? The simple answer might be: not concentrating on their business empire – because in 2008, it started to fall apart.

The company Dawnay, Day (from now on we will dispense with the comma) has an odd history. It was founded in 1928 by Julian Day and Guy Dawnay, and started out as an investment and finance business. In the 1970s the company was taken over by Lord Jacob Rothschild, before it was purchased in 1988 by Naggar as an empty shell. Klimt joined the Dawnay Day board in 1992.

Naggar and Klimt could not be more different, in terms of both upbringing and personalities. Born in Cannes, Naggar grew up in Paris, later studying engineering at the École Centrale. He trained as a merchant banker with Samuel Montagu & Co before moving to London in his 20s and becoming deputy chairman of Charterhouse Bank. Klimt, a Mumbai-born lawyer who specialized in tax, trained as a solicitor and became a partner at DJ Freeman, a London law firm. The pair met in the 1980s and started working together. Naggar concentrated his efforts on the finance side of the business, Klimt on the property side.

The recent history of the business is remarkable, not least for the extraordinarily varied and complex nature of its holdings. From a standing start, by 2007 the company claimed to have assets worth billions, although it is virtually impossible to put a definitive figure on the business because of the convoluted nature of its companies, holdings, subsidiaries and joint ownerships. Between them, Naggar and Klimt were at one point reported to have more than 500 directorships.

In the year 2000, Naggar was positioning the business as 'the UK's first internet-focused corporate finance and venture capital firm'. In 2005 it raised €375 million when it launched Dawnay, Day Treveria, an AIM-listed company, to invest in 75 German department stores. At one stage the property investment division supposedly had more than £2 billion of assets under management. Its UK property portfolio consisted of more than 400 commercial properties, totalling more than 7 million square feet in over 60 towns and cities, and in Europe the group had more than 40 commercial properties in Germany, Hungary, the Czech Republic and Poland.

Dawnay Day mc2 Capital Management was set up to manage the Global AdVantage Fund, a Dublin-listed hedge fund incorporated in the Cayman Islands. Dawnay Day bought the Caffe Uno chain from the Restaurant Group. This added to a previous deal to buy Paramount, the AIM-listed owner of the Chez Gerard, Bertorelli and Livebait chains, in a deal worth £28.9 million. Dawnay Shore hotels started buying up UK country house hotels.

In June 2007, Dawnay Day and Swordfish Investments completed the acquisition of Asquith Day Nurseries from Lyceum Capital for £95 million. Dawnay Day also invested in UK fashion chain Austin Reed. It also started to open offices in India for a planned expansion programme in which it was 'considering investing between $100 million and $200 million'. Oh, and it spent £130 million on 47 apartment blocks in Harlem, New York. And all this is only the tip of the Dawnay Day iceberg.

If it sounds confusing, it is meant to. Back-slapping media articles focused on how the firm had 'fingers in every pie', while Naggar dismissed accusations of a too rapid expansion programme by saying that people 'don't understand us'. But did they understand what they were doing? History would say not.

'You have to create an infrastructure,' explained Klimt to *Property Week* magazine in 2007. 'Without that, what you're doing is just a series of deals, a sequence of events – not creating a business.' Klimt went on modestly to explain, 'There are two guiding principles we've had all the way through. One is back talent. Two is buy hard assets with deep value. It's our way. We also like to have our own money in funds. We like to feel we're at risk.' But Klimt clearly did not take his own advice.

Speaking to former Dawnay Day employees, it is clear that Naggar and Klimt attracted some considerable talent to run the various businesses. But the approach does not suggest there was a particularly well-thought-out and prepared set of criteria in terms of operating the businesses. The basic idea was, do deals and make as much money as possible as quickly as they could. And while there is nothing wrong with this approach as such, it becomes a little harder to sustain when the credit dries up.

Some of those who came into direct contact with Klimt paint a picture of a thoroughly blunt individual. During a meeting between a relatively senior and new staff member, Naggar was apparently all smiles and informality. Klimt then strode into the room without knocking, requesting an immediate meeting with Naggar, while totally ignoring the new employee. When Naggar introduced the new person, Klimt offered a disdainful look and walked off. 'He likes you,' shrieked Naggar. They were something of an odd couple.

Klimt would also regularly tour guests around the various pieces of art hanging in the boardroom, irrespective of whether an important meeting was taking place. He would apparently stride right in and begin talking art, much to the horror of those chairing the important meetings. Klimt did not seem to care.

Klimt's bold claims of creating an infrastructure are completely dismissed by people who worked in the Dawnay Day empire. 'They were addicted to debt,' explained one, before adding: 'There was no such thing as a back office, apart from in terms of IT and HR, and little central control of the 80-plus businesses operating under the Dawnay Day name.' While it is not suggested that a good business must be run on the back of a McKinsey-style mission statement and the systematic integration of business units, the lack of coordination undoubtedly surprised many in the business. And the approach certainly added to the firm's woes when the going got tough.

Why was there no CEO of Dawnay Day to run the businesses as a coherent unit, and why was there not more integration, the use of economies of scale? There is no denying that the pair, through their chemistry and expertise, built and incredibly successful business. But it could be argued that the business might still be operating today if there had been a more coordinated approach and a greater structure.

In the same *Property Week* interview, Naggar bragged to the journalist that 'We don't even have a shareholders' agreement. We don't need one.' Those close to him question the sanity of such an arrangement. But for Naggar, it was all about the future. 'He was interested in what happened last month for about three seconds,' says a source. 'All he wanted to know about was next week, next month, the next deal.'

Since the firm's demise, commentators agreed that the business had 'an insatiable appetite for growth' which was ultimately to cause its demise. Others point to the character flaw that makes all people, not just Klimt and Naggar, constantly compare themselves with other, possibly wealthier or more successful, people in their peer group. It is a defect that, while driving growth, almost predestines people to ultimate failure.

The boardroom art was Naggar's big passion, and Dawnay Day's offices in London's Grosvenor Gardens, near Buckingham Palace, 'more closely resembled a private art gallery than a company HQ'. Naggar's wife Marion had a big part to play in this passion, and her family history offers an interesting side-story to the Dawnay Day debacle.

Marion Naggar comes from a wealthy background. Born Marion Samuel, part of the notable Samuel dynasty, her father, Lord Harold Samuel (or to give him his full title, Harold Samuel, Baron Samuel of Wych Cross), was the man who turned Land Securities into UK's first property company with more than £3 billion in assets. It did this by concentrating on the UK market rather than expanding overseas, something his son-in-law Naggar must now regret not having done.

The two have other things in common, though. Harold Samuel's initial success in the post-war property market was down to his shrewd business dealings and a love of subsidiaries. Until 1947, borrowing was limited to £10,000 unless permission to exceed this sum was given by a government body known as the Capital Issues Committee. For some years after 1947 money could not be borrowed without the consent of this body. Samuel overcame these problems by establishing subsidiaries, each of which could borrow up to the limit, and by taking over property companies that already had agreed borrowings.

Lord Samuel, incidentally, was supposedly the man who came up with the maxim, 'There are three things you need in property. These are location, location and location.'

Marion certainly inherited her father's love of art – it was probably difficult to escape it within the sumptuous confines of the stately family home at Wych Cross Place, East Sussex. Harold Samuel built up one of the finest collections of Dutch and Flemish paintings in the United Kingdom, since bequeathed to the Mansion House art collection. Marion and Guy continued the family tradition, and both were big on the art scene. Benefactors of (among others) the Tate museums, the Naggars were or are patrons, non-executives, 'friends' or trustees of a wide range of cultural, artistic and Jewish organizations, such as the Natural History Museum, the London Jewish Cultural Centre and even the hip and trendy Whitechapel Gallery in London's East End.

Naggar owned a Damien Hirst butterfly montage and a Tracey Emin wheelbarrow filled with rubbish and barbed wire (note to future, or overseas readers: this counted for art in the United Kingdom in 2008), while one of his more famous paintings was a Lucien Freud. In fact it was the sale of the Freud painting, called 'Benefits supervisor sleeping', that first brought concerns about the financial health of Dawnay Day to a wider public. It was sold in May 2008 at Christie's New York for US$33.6 million to Russian billionaire Roman Abramovich.

Although some cited Naggar's passion for art as one of the reasons behind the firm's downfall, the reality was that art was a hobby. If anything, the problem was less to do with the spending on art than with the impact it had on Naggar's business focus. Most commentators agree that the credit crunch, and Dawnay Day's debts, ultimately caused the company's collapse, but there was another key event, a tragic one, that had a massive impact.

In March 2008 Klimt's son was critically injured in a car crash in France. Klimt understandably dropped everything to be with his son. The problem was that he left everything in the hands of Naggar.

The fact was, Naggar and Klimt needed each other. The two were chalk and cheese, but they complemented each other and made up for each other's failings. Without Klimt, Naggar struggled to cope with poor markets and an unravelling, and sprawling, business empire. Rumours of their difficulties spread quickly, leading Dawnay Day's main lender, Norwich Union, now Aviva, to call in its £650 million loan to the company, secured on the property portfolio.

The firm's eventual undoing came after yet another move away from its core business into the trading of publicly listed stocks. A stake was built up in F&C Asset Management, on the premise that it would be sold by the parent company, Friends Provident, at a premium. Meanwhile the share price of the three AIM-listed property vehicles that Dawnay Day managed began to plummet as the commercial property sector slumped. But instead of pulling its cash out, Dawnay Day bought more shares in the market, using contracts for difference, on the assumption that the value of the assets would recover. It did not.

'It was a classic case of what so many people do in a bull market,' said one investor. 'They got carried away. But if your shares are going down and your margins are going up, you get a double whammy.' At one point, it is claimed that for every penny the shares fell, Naggar lost £1 million.

A former partner said, 'Their whole theory of how the world worked was wrong. They bet against everyone, exposed themselves more and more – and then caught a cold.' While this comment might be an oversimplification by a disgruntled former employee, it is remarkable that Klimt and Naggar were willing to bet everything they had created in 20 years on what seemed like a single punt on F&C. How on earth was that situation allowed to happen?

The complicated web of companies and subsidiaries controlled by Klimt and Naggar was ultimately proved to be something of a house of cards. 'The cross-share-holdings created a particularly toxic mix,' said one property analyst. The company was able to borrow vast amounts of money against its property portfolio, but when the price of property went down, the firm was caught short. Claer Barrett, who secured the first-ever joint interview with the two men, said, 'The basic modus operandi was driving debt to the maximum level on virtually everything they bought. In a rising market, taking on huge amounts of debt is the quickest way to expand.'

That was not quite how Barrett put it at the time of the interview in 2007, when she seemed dazzled by the 'extravagant art collection' and did not question the debt-driven strategy. Indeed, the now managing editor of *Property Week* magazine concluded the article with the words, 'Watch out, world.'

Watch out investors, she should have said. Of course using debt can work out well. Borrow £30 million, buy a business and sell it three years later for £100 million, and everyone is happy. Debt used astutely, judiciously and with insight is not a bad thing. But in this case, it was not.

The last board meeting at Dawnay Day was a sombre affair. Some of those attending were vitriolic in their opinion of Naggar, with some justification. The company had misrepresented itself up to the very end, and a lot of people had lost a lot of money as a result. Most of those in the room walked out without shaking his hand, and Naggar was visibly shaken by the turn of events. He could not believe that the business, and his own reputation, had collapsed so spectacularly. The philanthropist art dealer had managed to take the business from nothing to something and back to nothing in the space of 20 years.

While Naggar and Klimt probably will not have to worry too much about living on the breadline – many of the investment deals were shrewdly constructed with other people's money – people did lose their jobs as the firm went down, and of course some investors lost out big time. Of course the pair would have felt the collapse personally – they are not robots, after all – yet their personal wealth, while dented, would surely have softened the blow.

Naggar has been little seen since the demise of Dawnay Day. Klimt, meanwhile, has since started a new investment business. Another day, another dollar.

SOURCES

British Friends of the Art Museums of Israel, www.bfami.org
Business XL, February 2008
Daily Telegraph, 28 July 2008
Daily Telegraph, 4 October 2008
London Jewish Cultural Centre, www.ljcc.org.uk
Mansion House Art Collection, http://www.cityoflondon.gov.uk
Money Week, 8 August 2008
Natural History Museum, www.nhm.ac.uk
New York Times, 14 May 2008
PR Newswire, 11 January 2000
Property Week, 22 June 2007
Property Week, 20 March 2009
Sunday Times, 13 July 2008
Sunday Times, 3 August 2008
Tate Britain, www.tate.org.uk
The Times, 10 December 2005
The Times, 12 July 2008
The Times, 14 July 2008
The Times, 15 July 2008

www.altassets.com, August 19, 2005

www.amberleygroup.co.uk

www.business-standard.com, 31 May 2006

www.fundinguniverse.com/company-histories/Land-Securities-
 PLC-Company-History.html

www.investegate.co.uk/Article.aspx?id=200611101743109377L

www.london-gazette.co.uk/issues/58959/notices/714237

www.lyceumcapital.co.uk/pdfs/asquith_sale_070628.pdf

www.manfamily.org/PDFs/Harold%20Samuel%20Art%20
 Collection.pdf

www.secinfo.com

www.shorecap.co.uk

www.sleepdealer.com/presskit.pdf

www.thepeerage.com/p19180.htm

Film review quotes from *Time Out Chicago, New York Press, San
 Francisco Chronicle* and Nerve.com

Chapter Nine

Adolf Merckle
– One Step Too Far

It is hard to imagine exactly what thoughts were going through 74-year-old Adolf Merckle's head on Monday evening, 5 January 2009. Telling his wife Ruth that he was 'going into the office for a while', Merckle instead walked to the railway line near to his home, waited for the next train, and calmly stepped in front of it. It was a tragic end to an incredibly successful life.

Merckle was one of Germany's most successful and wealthy businessmen. In 2007, *Forbes* magazine reported he was worth US$12.8 billion, making him one of the wealthiest people on the planet. Under two years later, he would be dead.

Merckle was born in Dresden, Germany, in 1934. His grandfather had started a pharmaceutical business, called Drogen und Chemikalien en gros, in 1881 in Aussig, then part of the Austro-Hungarian Empire. His son Ludwig took over in 1915. Aussig was incorporated into the Third Reich in 1939, but after the Czech takeover in 1945 there was a German exodus, and the Merckles ended up in the small town of Blaubeuren in the state of Baden-Württemberg, in the south-western corner of Germany.

Adolf Merckle studied law in Germany and France, worked as a lawyer in Hamburg, and took over the pharmaceutical business founded by his grandfather in 1967. At the time it employed 80 people and had an annual turnover of DM4 million. Merckle was ambitious, and in 1973 he founded a business called Ratiopharm, Europe's first manufacturer of generic pharmaceuticals. It specialized in the production of well-known medicines whose patents had expired, meaning the company could offer the effective drugs at a cheap price. Business was good. Within a year of launching, revenues had increased tenfold. From offering 18 products in 1973, it now offers some 750, and the Ulm-based company operates in 35 countries and had a global turnover in 2008 of €1.9 billion.

In 1994 Merckle set up Phoenix Pharmahandel, a wholesale pharmaceuticals supplier. He did this by merging companies in Hamburg, Berlin, Mannheim, Nuremberg and Cologne, and at a stroke gained a 30 per cent market share. It is the largest pharmaceutical wholesaler in Germany, and the second largest in Europe, with about 20 distribution centres across the country delivering drugs to around 12,000 independent pharmacies. This is the sort of deal that only someone who lives, eats and breathes their business can do. No MBA graduate or experienced and professional CEO could have achieved this unless they had an entrepreneur's flair, drive and understanding of their business. This is what real vision looks like – Merckle should have been proud.

Yet this sort of genius also sowed the seeds of its undoing. Merckle will have believed that only he could have achieved this remarkable feat, but it cuts both ways. When times were tough, Merckle will have believed that only he could get himself out of the situation. So perhaps his thoughts that Monday evening were clear: all or nothing.

Merckle knew he was getting deeper and further into trouble. He had always been the master of his own destiny, fêted by the German and European business community. It was he who had built up this incredibly successful 100,000-employee conglomerate. He had made himself the fifth-richest man in Germany; nobody had done it for him, no advisor, no friend, not his wife, nor any colleague had achieved it for him. He was the master of this business.

Merckle bore witness to some incredible times in Germany's history. He was born just a few years before the Second World War, which was to be a devastating period for the country's economy. Yet from the ashes of defeat, Germany was reborn and rebuilt, becoming Europe's largest economy. Today it is the fifth largest economy in the world, although the burden of the 1990 reunification with East Germany has put a massive strain on the country, and it has expended considerable funds to bring Eastern productivity and wages up to Western standards. Its biggest problem is unemployment. While the overall rate hovers around 10 per cent, it rises to 30 per cent in some municipalities. Germany's export-orientated economy has also caused problems as weak global demand impacts on the country's businesses. These were just some of the issues Merckle had to contend with.

In 1997, Adolf Merckle handed over the day-to-day running of the business empire to his son, Ludwig. But Adolf could not let go, and he remained in the background and pulled the strings. His business ambition didn't stop at pharmaceutical businesses. He had stakes in myriad other firms, from a maker of grooming vehicles for ski slopes, to a sugar refinery, to one of Germany's oldest foundries. One of his biggest investments was in HeidelbergCement. Adolf's wife, Ruth Holland, was part of the Ulm cement dynasty Schwenk/Schleicher. The family have been shareholders in HeidelbergCement since 1911, and have been represented on the company's supervisory board since 1965. The Merckle family invested heavily in HeidelbergCement, a business that employs some 60,000 people at 2,600 locations in around 50 countries.

The core activity of HeidelbergCement is the production and distribution of cement and aggregates, the two essential raw materials for concrete. That is great when the world is busy building skyscrapers and new houses, less so in the teeth of a credit crunch and a global downturn in property prices.

In September 2007 the German business acquired rival Hanson plc, once one of Britain's most famous companies, making HeidelbergCement one of the largest companies of its type in the world. The £8 billion deal was the beginning of the end for Adolf Merckle. Financed through debt and on the verge of a global economic downturn that would hit the property sector particularly hard, in retrospect the deal looked doomed. But that would not be the end of Merckle's woes. If anything, it was only the entrée.

Doing a major deal just as the walls are closing in is a common characteristic for entrepreneurs on the edge. Yet often, the deal that is supposed to get the person out of the mess ends up being the deal that destroys the company – and the person.

While he was a God-fearing, conservative businessman, Merckle was a man of many faces. He could be jolly and friendly, but also merciless and puritanical. In a *Manager* magazine article, Merckle was once said to collect companies as others collect clocks, and he ran his business as if he lived in the 19th century. A former manager told the magazine that Merckle was 'greedy, envious and held grudges'. This greed was to be his undoing.

With credit drying up, Merckle turned to the money markets and attempted to gamble his way out of trouble through various investments. It was not the first time Merckle's risk-taking instincts took over, but it would be the last. He made a speculative investment based on his belief that Volkswagen shares would fall. He did this using so-called contracts for difference, and by short selling. But on 26 October 2008, Porsche announced it had secured stock and options equivalent to about 75 per cent of Volkswagen shares. The share price suddenly rocketed in two trading sessions, from €210 to just over €1,000, briefly making the auto maker the world's most valuable company by market capitalization.

It is estimated that Merckle took a €400 million hit on the shares, and his total losses ran to an eye-watering €1 billion. (In a piece of cruel irony, Porsche announced on Monday 5 January 2009, around the same time that Merckle was taking his own life, that it had acquired slightly more than 50 per cent of Volkswagen shares, and planned to buy 75 per cent of Volkswagen during the course of the year.) Clearly Merckle's deal was the wrong deal to do. But he was a brilliant, highly talented negotiator, someone who understood people and who had built fabulous wealth and success by doing things that he believed were the right things to do. Why give up on that faith in his abilities now? And in any case, would Merckle have taken advice even it were offered?

This amazing lack of commercial nous is pervasive among failing entrepreneurs. It is like a final flourish of virility before the curtain finally comes down. Merckle's judgement went from bad to worse. Did he really trust the Porsche family to sell him shares he needed to short VW? Did he not realize he was revealing his hand to a potential competitor and business adversary? Was he really in such a mess that he had to take this risk?

At a stroke, the 30 creditor banks financing the deal, including the likes of Commerzbank, Deutsche Bank and Edinburgh-based RBS, became nervous and demanded more security. Merckle, so long the man with the Midas touch, was starting to lose it. Former banking friends and allies became agitated about their exposure and turned their backs. Merckle's business empire was on the verge of being broken up. The prospects for his 100,000 employees suddenly looked bleak.

It was a bitter blow, and one compounded by the problems Merckle was having with the rest of his business empire. HeidelbergCement had debts of €12 billion, and his investment vehicle, VEM Vermögensverwaltung, owed up to €5 billion. Merckle himself could understand how he was being singled out.

In a rare interview with the leading German daily newspaper, *Frankfurter Allgemeine Zeitung*, Merckle complained about being compared with a hedge fund. 'The dealing we are now being criticized for we have for decades successfully accomplished,' he said:

> They were solidly calculated so that all our partners – businesses and also the banks – could profit from it. Yet now we are being thrown in the same pot as hedge funds, for what was a growth strategy for very respectable businesses. And our business partners also knew that.

Yet Merckle was acting like a hedge fund – and not like one that employed 100,000 staff. He continued to try to bluff it out. 'It is an unforeseeable situation,' he said, 'that despite our collateral, we have no access to credit.' Despite talking about how he and his business had survived previous stock market crashes, the reality was that Merckle was busy asking his local government in Baden-Württemberg for a bailout for his company. The news of his attempt to secure state aid went down badly.

'It is hard to believe that Merckle asks the taxpayer to redress his speculative mistakes,' wrote the *Frankfurter Allgemeine Zeitung*. 'Such a demand provokes rage. Every homeowner who cannot pay back the mortgage risks compulsory auction, regardless of whether her financial difficulties are her own fault or not.'

This case is not dissimilar to the claims made by fraudulent Wall Street financier Bernard Madoff to his investors the weeks before his house of cards collapsed. While it is not suggested that Merckle conducted his affairs in an illegal or fraudulent manner, it is worth noting that similar words and phrases are often used by legitimate entrepreneurs and those who are knowingly committing crimes. It is a very fine line.

As it happens, even his old friend Günther Oettinger, the minister president of Baden-Württemberg and the man who had recommended him for the Order of Merit, turned on Merckle. With Merckle requesting state help to save jobs, Oettinger called him a stockmarket gambler and refused to help.

The last weeks of Merckle's life were spent wrangling with a consortium of banks for a bridging loan that would tide over his investment vehicle, VEM. Realistically, though, it became obvious that Merckle would have to sell part or all of Ratiopharm, widely regarded as the family jewels.

So who was Adolf Merckle and what sort of man was he? Merckle's high-stakes stockmarket gambling was at odds with his conservative, patriarchal image. This was a man who cycled to work on an old bike, who travelled second class on the train and who drove an old Mercedes. He was a man who spent time hiking, in the Andes and Himalayas, and avoiding the limelight. Happily married with four children, Merckle was considered a classic Swabian – that is, someone from the south-west region of Germany, mockingly seen as tight-fisted. The joke among Germans is that an evening's entertainment for people from Baden-Württemberg is staying home and counting their money. It is true that Merckle had a long-running dispute with the tax authorities – it was even reported that he attempted to have a small fishing town, where he had a house, declared a tax-free zone.

But Merckle also endowed universities, supported a museum and had a collection of more than 4,000 works of art hanging on the walls of his various enterprises. He was fêted by politicians and sought out by bankers for his acumen. In Blaubeuren, he was seen as a man without airs and graces, ready to help out at village fêtes and generally known as Papa Merckle. The family was well respected locally, and in Blaubeuren there is even a street, Ludwig-Merckle-Straße, named after a family member.

Yet while he was lauded among his peers, it is fair to say that Adolf Merckle was not universally loved. 'Hardly a single other German corporate dynasty acts in such unpredictable and relentless way as the Merckle clan from Blaubeuren,' reported *Manager* magazine. While Merckle might have taken that as a compliment, it was not meant to be.

Yet Merckle did not set out to become the most popular businessman in Germany, even if he did become one of its most successful. Ultimately, in 40 years, Merckle's business empire became a world player with a turnover of more than €30 billion, employing more than 100,000 people. And while his worth dropped from US$12.8 billion in 2007 to US$9.2 billion in December 2008, he remained one of Germany's five richest men.

But it was not enough. 'The distress to his firms caused by the financial crisis and the related uncertainties of recent weeks, along with the helplessness of no longer being able to handle the situation, broke the passionate family businessman, and he ended his life,' the family said in a statement after his suicide.

Merckle was a Lutheran, which is a branch of Western Christianity that comes from the beliefs of 16th-century German reformer Martin Luther. It is big on predestination, meaning Lutherans believe all Christians are predestined for Heaven, which must have comforted Merckle on his walk to the railway line. Yet attitudes to suicide remain blurred for non-orthodox Christians, and it was completely outlawed (regarded as a religious sin, actually) until relatively recently. Today there is slightly more compassion for those committing suicide, and while not accepted, it is at least understood.

Apart from religion, though, the violence and selfishness of his suicide must have had a devastating impact on those around Merckle, particularly his family, whether he left a note or not. While suicide is often a desperate last act, it is hard to see why Merckle did not have alternatives.

Merckle's motto was 'Mir ist fremd, etwas aufzugeben' or 'It is alien to me to give up anything.' In the end, he gave up everything.

SOURCES

Bloomberg, 6 January 2009
Forbes magazine, 3 August 2007
Frankfurter Allgemeine Zeitung, 10 December 2008
Evening Standard, 6 January 2009
HeidelbergCement, www.heidelbergcement.com and www.heidelbergcement.com/uk/en/hanson/home.htm

Independent, 9 January 2009
New York Times, 7 January 2009
Ratiopharm, www1.ratiopharm.com/ww/en/pub/home.cfm
Sunday Times, 11 January 2009
The Times, 8 January 2009
www.stadt-blaubeuren.de

Chapter Ten

Boris Berezovsky
– Exile

In the 1990s, Boris Berezovsky had the ear of the then president of Russia, Boris Yeltsin. Having the ear of a heavy-drinking president might not, in retrospect, be that impressive, but with Yeltsin in charge of a global super-power, Berezovsky had influence by association. When Yeltsin's anointed successor took over, in the guise of Vladimir Putin, Berezovsky was expecting more of the same. He was wrong. Within days of coming to power in 2000, Putin promised to 'liquidate the oligarchs as a class'. And by oligarchs, he meant the likes of Berezovsky. While this move could be interpreted as a positive, pro-Western European approach to cleaner politics, others argue it was simply a way of clearing the field of other likely pretenders to the Putin throne.

Whatever the motive, Berezovsky took the hint. He fled to the United Kingdom where, perhaps oddly, he was granted British citizenship and from where he changed his name to Platon Elenin. Quite why the British government was prepared to accommodate such a character remains unclear. Questions on the subject to the British Foreign Office are rapidly dispatched with a curt 'no comment'.

Since 2001, Berezovsky has been provocateur number one, making threats to overthrow Putin, dismissing all manner of criminal allegations and fending off extradition orders to Russia. There remains an uneasy truce, although without doubt the Berezovsky story has further to run.

It is remarkable quite how far Berezovsky has come, but then has fallen. He was born in 1946, into a modest family in Moscow. A bright child, he went on to study forestry then applied mathematics, receiving a doctorate in computer science from Moscow State University in 1983, aged 37. He then worked on information management at the Academy of Sciences of the USSR before becoming a corresponding member of the Russian Academy of Sciences in 1991. His first foray into business was possible under the 'perestroika' period of Russian politics towards the end of the 1980s. Its literal meaning is 'restructuring', as in the restructuring of the Soviet economy, and these were heady times. Soviet leader Mikhail Gorbachev was behind the move towards 'demokratizatsiya', a form of political democratization, and the changes to Russian life would be deep and far-reaching.

One of the key economic reforms was the Law on Cooperatives, enacted in May 1987, which for the first time since Lenin permitted private ownership of businesses in the services, manufacturing, and foreign trade sectors. For those with entrepreneurial ambition, it was a green light.

Berezovsky's initial business dealings consisted of him and three friends going to West Germany, buying a used Mercedes and selling it on in Russia for three times what it cost. It didn't take a mathematician to work out that this was good business, and Berezovsky soon returned to Germany and came back with four more cars. There is no doubt that Berezovsky showed a healthy entrepreneurial flair. What is less clear is the means by which he managed to make it so big.

In 1992, he created LogoVaz, the USSR's first capitalist car dealership. It bought cars intended for export at the state-set prices, then sold them at the much higher prices to Russian consumers. 'We created the country's car market,' Berezovsky said. 'There was no market then.' Business boomed.

To achieve this level of business success, Berezovsky proved himself to be an expert political manipulator. In a country where making money was previously illegal, to have created such a massive car dealership business would not have been possible without friends in the right places. Berezovsky certainly had some nerve, but he wasn't finished with cars. With the Soviet government selling off state assets at knock-down prices and the now wealthy Berezovsky backing Soviet incumbent Boris Yeltsin, he flourished. In the chaotic fire sale of Russian state assets, Berezovsky managed to take ownership of the Sibneft oil company.

The business was created in 1995 by Presidential Decree 872, which ordered that the state's shares in oil-producing enterprise Noyabrskneftegas, the Omsk Refinery, exploration enterprise Noyabrskneftegasgeophysica and marketing company Omsknefteprodukt all be transferred to Sibneft. Berezovsky, along with fellow oligarch Roman Abramovich, bought the business through various front companies, for US$100 million. It was later valued at US$1 billion. He also took control of national airline Aeroflot, established a bank to finance his operations, and acquired several news media holdings, including stakes in television channels ORT and

TV6, and leading newspapers *Nezavisimaya Gazeta, Novye Izvestiya* and *Kommersant*.

Here was a real oligarch, straddling the worlds of politics, business and the media. He was the antithesis of what Putin wanted from his country's businesspeople, and it would put the two men on a collision course. It was by becoming a media baron that Berezovsky started to gain serious influence, and it was his 36 per cent stake in Russian public television channel ORT that became particularly important. The channel became an unofficial mouthpiece for the campaign to re-elect Boris Yeltsin. In 1996, Yeltsin's popularity rating was a miserable 30 per cent and his nationalist rival, Vladimir Zhirinovsky, was all set to defeat him. Then along came Berezovsky and his pro-Yeltsin propaganda machine, and the voters gave Yeltsin another four years. With the relief palpable in the capitals of Europe and beyond, Berezovsky was duly owed a few favours. He famously boasted how he was part of a small coterie of so-called oligarchs who owned 50 per cent of Russia's wealth. He was on top of the world, seemingly invincible.

First off he was given the mostly honorific post of deputy secretary of the National Security Council, then he became secretary of a Kremlin group coordinating the so-called Commonwealth of Independent States. Yet with Russian politics come intrigue, dark arts and the sort of plot lines only usually seen in a James Bond film. And it was in these posts that Berezovsky became embroiled in the murky and bloody civil war in Chechnya.

Situated in the extreme south-west of Russia, Chechnya occupies a mountainous region and borders Dagestan, Ingushetia and Georgia. It is a volatile part of the world, and one that has been fought over for centuries. In the 1990s, following the break-up of the Soviet Union, Chechnya went through two devastating wars, with separatists fighting Russian forces. Estimates put the total death toll from the first war (1994–96) at 100,000, and it was double or triple that for the second war (1999–2000). Today the republic is run by Ramzan Kadyrov, the son of former Chechen president Akhmad Kadyrov. Born in 1976, the Russian choice of leader is variously described as 'brutal, ruthless and anti-democratic'.

Berezovsky admitted that between 1997 and 1999, while he was an adviser to Yeltsin, he had had extensive contacts with Chechen separatist leaders, and that in 1997 he had given US$2 million of his own money to a Chechen field commander, Shamil Basayev, when Basayev was serving as Chechnya's prime minister. Basayev died in an explosion in 2006 – the Russians claimed they killed him, the Chechens said he died in an accidental explosion.

In the fog of war – particularly Russian ones – it is difficult to be sure quite what Berezovsky did or didn't do, but one thing is certain. When Putin came along as Yeltsin's successor, he presented himself as very much the tough-guy, pro-Russia and anti the Chechen 'rebels'. This posturing caught the mood of the public. And publicly, he wasn't best pleased with the likes of Berezovsky, who was quickly characterized as representing all that was wrong in post-Soviet Russia. For Berezovsky, who had helped Putin in his rise to power, it was quite a blow. Putin reportedly told some of Russia's big businessmen that they could do either business or politics, but not both. Sidelined, Berezovsky accused Putin of returning to totalitarianism. He also complained that the Kremlin had threatened him with imprisonment unless he surrendered control of television station ORT. He refused. Soon afterwards, an investigation into Berezovsky's handling of Aeroflot's finances was revived. He got the message – and fled to Britain.

It is hard to discern exactly why Berezovsky was prepared to risk everything he had accumulated to that point. All the work, the risks, the time and energy, all down the toilet and for what – to prove to the president that he was as tough as him? Or that he was an intellectual match? Did Berezovsky really harbour dreams of becoming Number One at the Kremlin – or did he assume he was untouchable? If so, he was badly wrong.

But he wasn't finished. In December 2000, he announced that he was establishing a New York-based, multi-million-dollar organization, the International Foundation for Civil Liberties, to promote judicial reform and the development of civil society in Russia. It is fair to say that this sort of effort did not go down well with the former KGB agent and judo expert Putin. He must have been furious. Battle lines were drawn. The fact that the British government made Berezovsky a British citizen did not smooth tensions, and ever since Berezovsky landed in the United Kingdom there has been a sort of tit-for-tat exchange of threats, abuses and claims.

Berezovsky was accused in Russia of defrauding a regional government of US$13 million. He strongly denied it. In 2007, a Moscow court found Berezovsky guilty of massive embezzlement while running Aeroflot, and sentenced him to six years in jail. Berezovsky called the accusations 'a farce' and again denied it. Also in 2007, Berezovsky told the British *Guardian* newspaper that he was plotting the violent overthrow of Putin. 'We need to use force to change this regime,' he said. 'It isn't possible to change this regime through democratic means. There can be no change without force, pressure.' Asked if he was effectively fomenting a revolution, he said, 'You are absolutely correct'. What a statement!

That, it is fair to say, went down like a ton of Chechen lead balloons in Moscow. Dmitry Peskov, the Kremlin's chief spokesperson, said at the time:

> In accordance with our legislation [his remarks are] being treated as a crime. It will cause some questions from the British authorities to Mr Berezovsky. We want to believe that official London will never grant asylum to someone who wants to use force to change the regime in Russia.

The British authorities kept schtum, at least publicly, and refused to hand over Berezovsky.

Now in his mid-60s, Berezovsky continues to antagonize from the wings, talking up his liberal-leaning credentials and the importance of limiting the power of the state. But while he has long predicted the end of Putin, it does not look like happening any time soon. Putin has since been succeeded by his preferred candidate, Dmitry Medvedev, in the role of Russian president while he remains very much involved under the title of prime minister.

Of course Putin would be wise not to ignore history. Just as he was appointed by the Yeltsin regime, Medvedev himself is now top man – and who knows what surprises the lawyer president from Leningrad will throw up.

And all the while, Berezovsky lives in the United Kingdom, travels with a retinue of heavies in bullet-proof vehicles and probably fears for his life. He has survived numerous assassination attempts, including a bomb that decapitated his chauffeur. He now has an office in Mayfair and an estate in Surrey, reportedly guarded by former members of the French foreign legion.

It's not only Russia that bears a grudge against Berezovsky. In 2007, a Brazilian judge issued an arrest warrant for him in relation to a money-laundering investigation. Berezovsky dismissed the investigation as a part of the Kremlin's 'politicized campaign' against him. In 2003, the Swiss financial authorities too investigated him for money laundering. Berezovsky claimed the proceedings were motivated by anti-semitism.

The Dutch authorities were said to have been investigating Berezovsky on similar charges, and then there are the accusations – unproven and hotly refuted – of his involvement in the murder of journalists. He was also closely associated with the former KGB agent Alexander Litvinenko, a man who came to a particularly Russian sticky end, poisoned by radioactive polonium-210.

While Berezovsky has never been found guilty of money laundering, and strongly denies any involvement with the death of Litvinenko and the journalists, these are not the sorts of things most entrepreneurs would wish to be associated with – unless they imagine themselves beyond the law. Berezovsky denies it all, talks of dark plots and claims political motivations are behind the charges.

So, Mother Teresa he is not. But what is he? While undoubtedly intelligent, occasionally charming, and an energetic entrepreneur, he blurred the line between business and politics and set off after both – something that has considerably affected his wealth, and may end up potentially damaging his health.

One journalist referred to him as 'a charming Machiavellian character whose drug is political intrigue'. Sergei Markov, a political consultant, described Berezovsky as a 'world-class provocateur... a character from Dostoevsky because he shows how intensive the dialogue can be between the human soul and the devil'. Vladimir Putin described him as – well, we can only imagine.

SOURCES

BBC News (2004) UK gives Russian tycoon new name [online] http://news.bbc.co.uk/1/hi/uk/3421883.stm (accessed 19 February 2010)

BBC (2005) Losing power: Boris Berezovsky, BBC News, 27 September [online] http://news.bbc.co.uk/1/hi/4286284.stm (accessed 17 February 2010)

BBC (2007a) Russian dissident Boris Berezovsky blames the Russian president for the murder of former KGB agent Alexander Litvinenko, 31 May [online] http://news.bbc.co.uk/2/hi/europe/6708103.stm

(accessed 19 February 2009)

BBC (2007b) Moscow court convicts Berezovsky, 29 November [online]

http://news.bbc.co.uk/1/hi/world/europe/7118660.stm (accessed 17 February 2010)

Cobain, I, Taylor, M and Harding, L (2007) I am plotting a new Russian revolution, *Guardian*, 13 April 2007 [online] http://www.guardian.co.uk/world/2007/apr/13/topstories3.russia (accessed 17 February 2010)

Dejevsky, M (2006) Boris Berezovsky: the first oligarch, *Independent*, 25 November

Forbes (1996) Godfather of the Kremlin, 30 December [online] http://www.forbes.com/forbes/1996/1230/5815090a.html (accessed 19 February 2010)

Hearst, D (2007) Fortune made in Yeltsin era, *Guardian*, 13 April

Jones, L (2007) My dinner with Boris Berezovsky, *The First Post*, July 20, 2007 [online] http://www.thefirstpost.co.uk/7865,news-comment,news-politics,my-dinner-with-boris-berezovsky (accessed 17 February 2010)

Jordan, M and Finn, P (2006) Russian billionaire's bitter feud with Putin a plot line in poisoning, *Washington Post*, 8 December

Marsh S (2007) Berezovsky is playing us, and it's embarrassing, *The Times*, 30 July [online] http://www.timesonline.co.uk/tol/comment/columnists/guest_contributors/article2156186.ece (accessed 17 February 2010)

Ritchie, M (2002) Billionaire's tale is Russian hit, BBC News, 2 October, 2002 [online] http://news.bbc.co.uk/1/hi/entertainment/2290059.stm (accessed 17 February 2010)

Sunday Times (2007) Profile: Boris Berezovsky, 15 April [online] http://www.timesonline.co.uk/tol/life_and_style/men/article1654881.ece (accessed 17 February 2010)

Wikipedia (nd)

International Foundation for Civil Liberties

www.worldbank.org

Chapter Eleven

Zhou Zhengyi
– Power Politics

In 2002, *Forbes* magazine listed 41-year-old Chinese property developer Zhou Zhengyi as the 11th richest man in China. In a population of 1.3 billion, that made him richer than 1,299,999,989 other Chinese people. That was pretty good going for the Shanghai-born Zhou, whose start in business came in 1978 as the teenage owner of a wonton noodle restaurant in the Yangpu district of the city. To put it in perspective, the purchasing power of his millions is worth around 10 times the amount in China itself, making the sheer scale of Zhou's achievement much more remarkable than most Western rags-to-riches story. And when you add into the mix that it was created under the all-powerful glare of the omnipotent Communist party, it is all the more incredible still – especially in a society that promotes community spirit and acting for the good of all. His entrepreneurial tendencies would normally have been crushed at birth.

But of course, times are changing in China. Zhou's meteoric rise to prominence in China, and particularly Shanghai, was phenomenal, and the name 'Zhou' was generally prefaced with the words 'flamboyant' and 'entrepreneur'. He was young, smart, successful and wealthy, was part of the jet-set of Shanghai elites – and he had a beautiful wife. Then in 2008, he was sentenced to 16 years in prison for bribery and embezzlement.

It was a case that went to the very top of the Communist Chinese government and led to the dismissal of Shanghai's Communist Party chief Chen Liangyu. And while no one is disputing the extraordinary rise of China, the case of Zhou Zhengyi exposed the corruption that is one of the problems at the root of the country's phenomenal growth.

Shanghai has been in existence for more than 1,000 years, and its location at the mouth of the Yangtze River, roughly equidistant from Beijing and Hong Kong, means it has long been an important trading crossroads. Today, Shanghai is the largest city in China in terms of population and one of the largest metropolitan areas in the world, home to more than 21 million people. From being the largest economic and transportation centre in China – in 2005 it became the world's largest cargo port – Shanghai is now busy striving to turn itself into one of the world's greatest economic, financial, trade and transportation hubs.

Its economic importance to China has long given Shanghai big political clout. The Chinese Communist Party was formed in Shanghai in 1921, while Mao Zedong, the first chairman of the Communist Party of China, cast the first stone of the Cultural Revolution in the city by publishing political rhetoric he had been unable to get published in Beijing. Even today, those in Shanghai's top jobs, such as the party chief and the position of mayor, are always prominent on a national scale. Indeed, four secretaries of the municipal

Party committee, or mayors from Shanghai, eventually went on to take prominent central government positions, including former president Jiang Zemin, former premier Zhu Rongji, and current vice president Xi Jinping.

Over the past 20 years Shanghai has expanded sixfold, an incredible rate but one that has come at a cost. The huge road-expansion plans conceived in the 1980s predicted that Shanghai would top 2 million cars in 2020 – a figure it surpassed in 2004. And while it boasts more skyscrapers than New York, the city's building practices, in terms of style, quality and dubious town planning decisions, leave much to be desired. In June 2009, a just-completed 13-storey block of flats collapsed, raising fresh questions about corruption and shoddy practices in China's construction industry. While it is easy to point fingers, no nation is innocent when it comes to corruption and political interference, especially in the so-called advanced West. And of course, corruption or not, the Chinese growth miracle has taken hundreds of millions out of poverty.

Into this rapidly expanding world of opportunities was born Zhou Zhengyi (also, confusingly for Western readers, known as Chau Ching-ngai). One of seven children, he was born into a tough, waterfront area of Shanghai by the Huangpu River. Zhou dropped out of secondary school to open a noodle bar, and went on to open two smarter restaurants in the city, a karaoke bar and a sauna. But Zhou saw the impending building boom all around him and was soon investing his profits in a building materials business. Despite communism, China still managed to nurture a culture of entrepreneurship. By the early 1990s Zhou was trading in copper futures and other commodities on the London and Shanghai exchanges. But the big bucks were in property in Shanghai, where land was controlled by the state and private developers were clamouring to cash in on the government's economic reforms. And Zhou, who counted Chen Liangjun, the brother of the former Shanghai party secretary, as an associate, soon did exactly that.

Zhou's ability to harness the communist political infrastructure to further his own entrepreneurial ends was impressive. And all this in a country where there is a tangible reverence and a general desire to 'fit in' and not to rock the boat. Zhou's property dealings saw him amass a US$320 million fortune – enormous by normal Chinese standards. But that was not made through simply working hard and being nice to his employees. As the friendship with Chen Liangjun highlights, it is not just hard work that gets you to the top in China – it is who you know. And Zhou knew a lot of people.

His trouble started, though, when demolition men banged on the doors of some old apartment buildings in the prime West Beijing Road area of Shanghai. The 2,159 residents had little alternative but to move out, but they did not go quietly. Residents claimed they had received inadequate compensation (as little as £10,000 each in a city where properties cost a small fortune) and had suffered violent intimidation. Lawyer Zheng Enchong agreed to act for them and, on 28 May 2003, at the Jingan District People's Court in Shanghai, the case opened.

The lawsuit was from six homeowners representing 2,159 original residents. The plaintiffs claimed that the Jingan District Property Development Bureau, under the instructions of the district government, improperly allowed a company controlled by Zhou to redevelop the 43,000 square metre property without paying a land lease with an estimated value of US$36.3 million. The case did not go well. Eight days after bringing the action, the lawyer was arrested, charged with 'disclosing state secrets' and sentenced to three years in jail! As for the case, it was dismissed. But the residents were not having it. Outraged, they took their grievances to party leaders in Beijing. The result of such militancy: 85 of them were arrested as they tried to deliver a petition.

Yet while the Beijing authorities clamped down on these particular Shanghai residents, they were obviously becoming increasingly exasperated with the likes of Zhou and the so-called 'Shanghai faction'. Soon after the West Beijing Road affair, Zhou was charged and found guilty of stock market fraud and falsifying registered capital reports. He was arrested in connection with a Y2 billion (US$242 million, or £132 million) loan he obtained from the Bank of China for his unlisted property company, New Nongkai Global Investments. It was a case that was to have repercussions, not least for the bank, the fifth-largest in China. It turned out that the Bank of China had failed to follow proper procedures in making various loans to Zhou: one was granted on the same day as the application, without the pledging of any security, something unheard of for ordinary Chinese people.

The vice-chairman and chief executive of Bank of China (Hong Kong), Liu Jinbao, was duly arrested and charged with bribery among other things. He has not been seen since. There were also shady goings-on at Zhou's Shanghai Land business, involving him and his glamorous wife Sandy Mo (also known as Mao Yuping or Mo Yuk-ping). She was arrested and charged for defrauding five banks of HK$89 million using bogus letters of credit. Although she denied the charges, she got a three-year prison sentence.

Yet while Western readers may think Zhou's three-year detention is punishment enough, the length of his sentence was met with incredulity from sections of Chinese society. In a country where the death sentence is routinely meted out in corruption cases, Zhou got off very lightly indeed, leading to talk of a plea bargain – and of friends in high places. According to Amnesty International, China carried out more executions than the rest of the world put together in 2008. Even on percentage terms, it rates higher than the United States, itself not averse to the practice. Since 1 January 2007 China has required the Supreme Court to review all death sentences, although the exact number of people executed is classified as a state secret. The death penalty still applies to 60 offences in China, including non-violent crimes such as tax fraud and embezzlement – meaning the likes of Zhou must have been confident in their connections.

That said, the Chinese state is conscious of outside pressures on the subject, and in July 2009 Zhang Jun, vice-president of the Supreme People's Court, said the court would in future impose more 'suspended death sentences'. Other gossip relating to Zhou's case touched on the politics at work and the power struggles between Hu Jintao (the current general secretary of the Communist Party of China), Wen Jiabao (the current premier of the People's Republic of China) and the Shanghai faction headed by former president Jiang Zemin.

Zhou was a friend of the so-called 'princelings', or children of the powerful Shanghai faction, but these relationships meant he was on the other side to Hu and Wen. Imprisoning Zhou was seen by many as Hu and Wen's way of taking the Shanghai faction down a notch. And it would not be the last time.

Zhou's lenient sentence was not a lesson to him. Soon after his release in 2006 he was arrested again for his involvement in a property scandal that misappropriated millions of dollars from Shanghai's social security fund. This time, the scandal went to the very top of the Shanghai elite – and the powers that be in Beijing decided they had had enough. Heads would roll. The investigation uncovered a complex web of corruption, bribery and embezzlement that reached every corner of business and politics in Shanghai.

Among those who stood trial were Ling Baoheng, Shanghai's former chief watchdog of state-owned assets. He was charged with taking bribes totalling Y500,000. Other people involved included highway tycoon Liu Genshan, Wu Hongmei, former deputy director of the Shanghai Municipal State-owned Assets Supervision and Administration Commission, and Yin Guoyuan, former deputy director of Shanghai Housing, Land and Resources Administration.

By far the biggest scalp was Chen Liangyu, who sat on the 24-man ruling politburo as well as running China's largest city. Hundreds of millions of pounds had been siphoned out of the city's pension fund, and Chen was accused of cronyism, covering up offences by staff, and nepotism. For someone of Chen's standing to face legal trouble is exceedingly rare in China, even if the authorities have evidence of corrupt activities by them or people close to them. Actions like these do not happen unless they are sanctioned from the very top. President Hu Jintao wanted it known that he was prepared to crack down on graft – particularly if his political opponents are involved.

Again it was part of a broader political tussle about control of the Communist Party and the government. The message was that Beijing is very much in control, and that it would not put up with the likes of Chen and Zhou doing what they wanted.

Yet for Zhou, old habits die hard. In addition to the embezzlement charges, Zhou was charged with bribing prison authorities to gain special privileges, including conducting business meetings and making phone calls from prison. Incredibly, Yu Jinbao, a supervisor in the Shanghai Tilanqiao prison, was sentenced to two years in prison for writing more than 200 letters to try to get Zhou's sentence commuted! Others were done for accepting gifts from 'Zhou's people'. In a neat conclusion to that part of Zhou's story, four of his jailers were eventually jailed for corruption.

Zhou's story shows how success can be dangerous game in China. Intertwined with politics, power games, a disregard for the law, nepotism, bribery and corruption, it is an issue that the authorities realize could continue to be a serious problem in the future.

Zhou's case smacks of a certain arrogance, brought about by such amazing success from an early age. It was not that Zhou thought he was untouchable because of who he was (after all, he was a nobody, really). It was more than he felt untouchable because of his achievements and wealth. It is a self-belief bordering on delusion. Zhou's greatest mistake was not realizing that the wind in China can quickly change direction.

SOURCES

Amnesty International
BBC, 1 June 2004
Bloomberg, 29 November 2007
Business Week, January 2009
China Daily, 23 December 2004
China Daily, 11 August 2007
China Daily, 7 January 2008
Daily Telegraph, 26 September 2006
Financial Times, 21 February 2004
Financial Times, 8 July 2004
Financial Times, 15 July 2005
Financial Times, 30 November 2007
Guardian, 25 September 2006
International Herald Tribune, 25 September 2006
Lonely Planet

People's Daily, 29 June 2007
People's Daily, 22 January 2008
People's Daily, 15 July 2008
Standard (Hong Kong), 3 June 2004
Standard (Hong Kong), 14 May 2005
Standard (Hong Kong), 27 May 2006
Sunday Times, 6 June 2004
http://shanghaiist.com, 27 June 2006

Chapter Twelve

Mark Goldberg
– Paying the Penalty

In June 1998, multi-millionaire IT recruitment entrepreneur Mark Goldberg fulfilled his boyhood dream and became owner of south-London-based Crystal Palace Football Club. He had big dreams for the club to compete at the very top of European football, alongside the likes of Arsenal and Manchester United.

From the start, he meant business. He hired a former England football manager, Terry Venables, to run the club, and was soon splashing the cash on exotic international players. Goldberg also invested in the club's training facilities, spending thousands on furniture and equipment, hiring a full-time club doctor and installing a new level of management in the club to cover IT functions, human resources and public relations. He even hired an internet specialist to help promote the club in China.

Unfortunately for Goldberg and Palace, in between his registering an interest and actually taking the reins at the club, it was relegated to the second tier of British football – a devastating financial blow. Unperturbed, Goldberg continued to talk up the potential of the club, and even floated the idea of buying British football legend Paul Gascoigne to join this south London revolution.

It was not to be. Gascoigne never came, Venables soon left in acrimonious circumstances, and within a year the club was put into administration with debts of £30 million. Goldberg was soon declared bankrupt.

The most astonishing aspect of the case is the speed with which it unravelled. It is quite extraordinary the way he managed to fritter enough money to last several lifetimes. From sitting on a £40 million fortune, Goldberg managed to lose the lot in less than 18 months.

Goldberg was entrepreneurial from a young age. The son of a south London dentist, he used to buy fruit from wholesalers and sell it on at markets. He bought and sold a range of goods, even cars, although the experience would prove a bad omen. 'I bought [the cars] because I liked them,' he says, 'rather than because they were good cars. I remember buying a BMW 2002, the old model, with the little round back lights – I think I spent £400 and ended up needing a completely new reconditioned engine, which cost another £600. I think in the end I had to give it away.' Goldberg is plainly different: a serial entrepreneur who does not learn from his mistakes.

Away from business, Goldberg also showed a passion for football. When he was 18, he won a soccer scholarship to the College of William and Mary in Williamsburg, Virginia, but dropped out because of a recurring hamstring injury. It was a passion that stayed with him, though, becoming something of an unhealthy obsession.

When Goldberg returned from America, he worked in a recruitment business in London. A quick learner, he soon realized there was a growing demand for IT specialists. He also realized that companies were prepared to pay agencies hefty finders' fees. This ability to learn quickly and work out ways of generating revenue is vital for successful entrepreneurs. Goldberg wasted no time at all, and his firm, MSB International, started cashing in.

MSB would find qualified IT specialists and put them together with the people who needed them. It would pay the IT people £1,000 a week and charge the client £1,200. Each contractor Goldberg could place made him £200 a week. And by 1986, when Goldberg was 23, he had 25 contractors, making him £20,000 a month. He soon realized that if could train up people to do his job, the money would start flooding in. And it did. Fifteen years after starting the business it employed 150 sales people and handled 2,500 IT contractors.

Goldberg floated the business in 1996, but the company really started doing well as Y2K computer fears heightened. Towards the end of the decade, the business world was rife with fears that come midnight on the evening of 31 December 1999, computer systems around the globe would collapse, bringing the world to its knees. Companies such as MSB made the most of those fears. Revenues rose from £18 million to £129 million in the three years to 1998. The share price followed suit, quadrupling from the float price to more than 1,000p in the same year. Goldberg made something like £40 million. But he was about to lose the lot.

As Goldberg's wealth grew, he invested some of it in his favourite football club, Crystal Palace. By December 1997 he had £3 million worth of shares, a seat on the board, and was 'an active, enthusiastic director' of the club. He also believed that he could use his business acumen to make Palace, as it is known to its supporters, one of the most successful football clubs in the land. It was a classic error of judgement: applying sound principles from one business or sector to a completely different industry. It shows an incredibly blinkered vision, and one doomed to failure.

Goldberg was instrumental in the purchase of footballers Attilio Lombardo and Michele Padovano from the Italian football giant Juventus. He also let it be known to the incumbent chairman, Ron Noades, that he would be prepared to buy the club if it was up for sale. Noades the butcher spotted Goldberg the lamb. What was to follow was pure slaughter.

Noades made Goldberg a ridiculous offer: to sell him the club and its Selhurst Park stadium for £30 million. For a club on the verge of relegation it was an extortionate amount, but Goldberg agreed. He went off to find potential investors, but returned to Noades saying he could only raise around £22.8 million.

Noades then suggested that Goldberg could purchase just the club but not the stadium (Noades agreed to lease the stadium to Goldberg). Again, incredibly, Goldberg agreed to these terms. However, it soon came to light that Goldberg had only managed to raise £18 million – so Noades himself ended up loaning Goldberg the outstanding £5 million! And actually, the potential investors had also got cold feet, leading Goldberg to sell most of his stake in MSB and use his own money to buy the club. Noades agreed to let Goldberg pay him in instalments over five years.

In reality, without the freehold of the ground, the deal left Goldberg with negligible assets. Noades later stated that Goldberg had been 'stupid' to buy the club – adding, 'He wet his knickers about buying the place.' Not the strongest bargaining position, then.

But bargaining and negotiating are what recruitment consultants are supposedly good at. What on earth was

Goldberg doing, and how could he have been so blinded by his love of football and this football club? The naivety of youth can be the only reason. Here was Goldberg, who had just made a fortune. What could possibly go wrong?

It is a good question who, if anyone, was advising Goldberg on his football folly. Regardless, the deal went through and Goldberg was installed as chairman. It was a dream come true that was about to turn into a nightmare. After the deal was done, Noades famously gave Goldberg a gift: a Porsche. Goldberg later commented, 'I worked it out later that the Porsche cost me about £37 million and was the most expensive car ever sold on the planet.'

Goldberg's first act was to move long-serving manager Steve Coppell to director of football. He then installed Italian Attilio Lombardo and the soon-to-retire Tomas Brolin as player-managers, something football observers referred to with some understatement as 'strange'. Not only was Lombardo one of the club's key players, he didn't even speak English. The arrangement did not last, but in an even more eccentric move, Goldberg appointed former owner Ron Noades, alongside coach Ray Lewington, as caretaker manager.

The club was relegated from the Premier League, finishing bottom of the table. But Goldberg had not even started. In his bid to make Crystal Palace one of the nation's leading teams, he installed former England head coach Terry Venables as manager.

While Venables, or El Tel as he is known to the British tabloids, was and to some extent remains a favourite with the fans, he also courted controversy. In January 1998, the High Court in London banned him from being a company director for seven years. In their case against Venables, the Department of Trade and Industry outlined instances of bribery, lying, deception, manipulation of accounts and taking money that should have been given to creditors. Although the case was set to take three weeks, the fact that he decided to admit or not contest 19 specific allegations made against him meant it was over in five minutes.

Much later the details of his audacious appointment as Palace manager came to light. Again, you have to wonder where Goldberg was getting advice. First of all it was claimed that Goldberg paid Venables £135,000 just to talk about becoming the Crystal Palace coach! He went on to agree a deal with Venables that saw him pocket £750,000 salary per year after tax, to be paid annually – in advance. Venables also got an unsecured £500,000 interest-free loan, a £650,000 house, a Mercedes car, a 10 per cent pension contribution and £20,000 in relocation expenses (he was then the head coach of Australia).

Goldberg also allegedly promised Venables millions in the way of money that could be used on player signings, and a 5 per cent bonus on amounts not spent on transfers. He also agreed that Venables could remain as a consultant to the Australian Football Association, and that El Tel was entitled to a 6 per cent royalty on the use of his image.

'To my mind, [Venables] is the only man who can give the team the confidence they need,' Goldberg said at the time. Jim McAvoy, the club's former chief executive, later added, 'Mark made the astonishing statement that he didn't want anyone to think that he couldn't afford Terry Venables.'

It wasn't one of salesman Goldberg's best deals. Although come the following season the team, under Venables, started to improve, the transfer policy under Goldberg was chaotic. Players were offered crazy (for the time) signing-on fees and silly wages. Players were offered three- or four-year deals, and there were even loyalty bonuses for those who stayed at the club. The signing of Yugoslav international defender Gordan Petric summed up the confused approach at the time. While a good player, he cost £300,000 and was on a £5,000 per week deal. The thing was, the club had at least nine other senior players who could play in central defence, so his skills really were not needed.

For the club's hierarchy, though, according to former chief executive Jim McAvoy, it was the fees paid to the players' agents that were most galling. He claimed agents were paid more than £1 million during Goldberg's reign. 'Negotiations with agents and the manner by which players were being identified, brought to the club on trial, was completely unprofessional,' McAvoy said later in a leaked letter to his fellow directors. 'I have no doubt we were seen as an easy touch. All of this undermined the credibility of the club.'

McAvoy was specific about three Argentineans signed by the club, Pablo Rodrigues, Christian Ledesma and Walter Del Rio. 'The Argentinean escapade cost £448,769 in agent fees and £187,000 in transfer fees,' McAvoy said. Del Rio's contract was terminated in March after one first-team start and one substitute appearance, while Rodrigues and Ledesma were never signed.

Goldberg blamed Venables, and Venables, who had been around football long enough to see the impending train crash coming, decided to pack his bags and left. In total he lasted little more than seven months at the club – a deal that ended up costing Goldberg something like £1 million for each month.

Spending was no less prolific off the pitch. When Goldberg took over, he made a series of appointments at the Selhurst Park-based club. He appointed a broadcasting manager, an IT manager, a human resources manager, an 'internet specialist' and a variety of other public relations executives, on annual salaries estimated between £30,000 and £50,000. Goldberg also spent 'hundreds of thousands of pounds' on furniture, computers and training equipment, but the biggest expense was staff, including a full-time doctor (estimated salary £100,000), a fitness expert and team of personal trainers, a nutritionist (another £100,000), various physiotherapists, a masseur – and even a cook.

One of the most poignant comments about Goldberg's spending came from former manager, the softly spoken Steve Coppell. 'He bought hundreds of gallons of bottled water. Under Ron Noades, we just filled bottles from the tap.'

Goldberg was spending money like water, and it could not – and would not – continue. The club's relegation cost it dear – around £3.5 million from Sky TV, £280,000 from Carling sponsorship, £182,000 in overseas broadcasting rights, £33,000 of radio revenue, and more than £24,000 for every *Match of the Day* show. And with falling gate receipts and less of an appeal for the club merchandise, circumstances combined to add more woe.

Goldberg was soon paying the players' wages (£500,000 each month!) from his own pocket, and financial armageddon loomed. Goldberg defaulted on his £67,000-a-month loan repayment to Ron Noades (who promptly sued). The club finally went into administration in March 1999 with debts of £30 million. Goldberg was declared bankrupt nine months later.

It is hard not to sympathize with Goldberg, regardless of this ludicrous football foray. He was not setting out to rob or defraud, after all. All he wanted was to make Crystal Palace one of the best clubs in the land – and do so with his own money. It is clear he was unprepared for the massive and constant drain on his resources.

It all meant that Goldberg was barred from being a company director for at least two years. He lost his villa in Marbella, his assets, shares, cash, reputation and it even caused his marriage to fail. He literally blew it all.

The Crystal Palace affair was not his only legal wrangle. A dispute with former business partner Peter Browne over a property deal also ended up in the courts. Again Goldberg was found wanting. The high court judge Justice Jacobs branded Goldberg 'dishonest' and a 'liar'. At one stage he said, 'I have already stated that Mr Goldberg is not to be trusted.'

Throughout all his difficulties, though, Goldberg has remained remarkably upbeat. Although bankrupted, he was soon embarking on a new recruitment-based venture, called TV Jobshop, although he was at pains to point out (especially to his creditors) that he was merely the sales and marketing manager. 'I don't direct the business,' he said in one newspaper interview, 'I drive the business' – whatever that means. More recently Goldberg has been talking up a new property-related business venture. 'I'm hoping to build a couple of sports villages in the UK before the 2012 Olympic Games,' he has said.

Day to day, Goldberg has returned to football by becoming manager of Bromley Football Club, a Kent-based outfit operating in the Conference South league. While he got the job on the back of his brother-in-law being chairman, Goldberg's football record is good. 'I'm much happier in the dugout than in the boardroom and maybe that's what I always wanted,' he says. 'But it was never going to happen at Palace. The next best thing was to own the club and to have some sort of control over the football but it's the football I love, not the chairmanship.'

In terms of how and where it all went wrong for him, Goldberg is refreshingly frank. 'I had a number of investors with me who had promised to put money in,' he says. 'Foolishly, I put my money up first on the basis that they were going to follow.' He also admits that he did not expect the salaries to spiral out of control the way they did, and third, he says he thought he could handle the club's hefty debt when he couldn't.

'I wasn't unlucky,' he says.

> I was too eager to do the deal. I wanted it too badly. In a
> way, I deserved what I got because I let my heart rule my
> head. I would do things a lot differently if I was in that
> position again but I don't regret what I did. I did fulfil a
> lifetime ambition of owning the football club I supported
> as a boy. But I really did lose £40 million of my own money,
> and I really did do it with the right intentions.

He admits he was naïve in terms of the Venables situation,
but again puts it down to youthful enthusiasm.

But losing £40 million wasn't good, he says. He:

> had to sell a number of lovely houses. It was stressful for the
> family. I remember people sitting in my kitchen with their
> heads in their hands waiting for me to walk through the
> door. I said: 'Look, no one's died. Look at my dad, he's been
> through two triple bypass operations and he's still with us.
> This is nothing to cry over.

While Goldberg remains sanguine about losing the money
('there is only a certain amount of money that you actually
need'), it has not stopped him dusting himself down and
looking towards the future. 'I lost my entire wealth but I
didn't lose the ability to work hard,' he says. 'All of your
materialistic possessions can vanish but you always have
the knowledge of how you built every brick of the business
that generated those materialistic things in the first place.'

Throughout it all, Goldberg says he has learned valuable
lessons in business and life. 'I've sought great success,' he
says.

> I've experienced great success. I've also experienced taking
> very large risks, and I've experienced the occasions when
> the risks turned into a success. Large risks can often result

in a greater fall. I have seen extremes. I have built a business from scratch from a desk with a phone into a £200-million company.

Finally, he adds:

When I was chairman I was a little bit in awe of what was going on. I've been an example of how you can take knocks in life and bounce back. If anything I would like my kids to be proud of me and I would never want the Crystal Palace story to be the last chapter.

Fair play to him: the man has heart.

SOURCES

BBC, 11 October 2000
BBC, 12 May 2008
Daily Telegraph, 8 October 2000
Daily Telegraph, 12 January 2001
Guardian, 13 October 1999
Guardian, 11 November 2006
http://networkersmsb.com
Independent, 28 April 1999
Independent, 31 July 1999
Independent, 25 June 2000
Independent, 2 April 2005
Recruiter magazine, 9 December 2003
Sunday Times, 28 December 2003
The Times, 31 July 2006
www.altonwood-group.co.uk
www.bfctv.co.uk
www.cpfc.co.ukwww.fool.co.uk, 4 April 2000
www.londonstockexchange.com
www.surreylife.co.uk

Chapter Thirteen

Ken Lay
– Friends in High Places

Ken Lay's memorial service was some event. More than 1,000 mourners gathered on Wednesday 12 July 2006 at the First United Methodist Church, Houston, including former president George Bush and his wife Barbara, and former US secretary of state James Baker. Also present were ex-secretary of commerce Robert Mosbacher, former Enron president John Seidl, and Drayton McLane, owner of the Houston Astros baseball team.

The Reverend William Lawson, a Houston civil rights leader, addressed the congregation with some strong words, likening Lay to James Byrd, a black man who was dragged to death in a racially motivated murder near Jasper, Texas, in 1998. 'Ken Lay was neither black nor poor, as James Byrd was,' said Lawson, 'but I'm angry because Ken was the victim of a lynching'.

A friend of the Lay family went on to describe Ken as a 'good, honest, God-fearing friend who did not have a criminal bone in his body.' He added: 'What really makes me sad today... is that Ken may not be remembered for these enviable qualities. Instead, many will remember him for the Enron bankruptcy, the indictment and the trial. Overzealous federal prosecutors and media have vilified an exceedingly good man'.

It is more likely than not that Lay will be remembered for his criminal role in the bankruptcy of the once-mighty Enron Corporation, of which he was head man. Found guilty, alongside former Enron chief executive Jeffrey Skilling and others, of conspiracy and fraud, Lay was due to be sentenced when he died of heart failure in Aspen, Colorado, on 5 July 2006. He was 64.

Kenneth Lee Lay was born in 1942 in Tyrone, Missouri, a so-called bellwether state in the United States on account of its mirroring the demographic, economic and political make-up of the nation. It was a modest upbringing. Lay's father was a Baptist minister and tractor salesman, but the pair shared a work ethic and intellect.

Lay was president of his fraternity at the University of Missouri, where he graduated with economics qualifications in 1965. He then worked as an economist at Exxon Mobil, before successfully completing a PhD in economics at the University of Houston, Texas, in 1970. This was a man who understood numbers.

Before embarking on his business career, Lay turned to politics. He was a technical assistant to the commissioner of the Federal Energy Regulatory Commission and later deputy under secretary for energy of the US Department of Interior. Also while in Washington, Lay was an assistant professor at George Washington University, teaching graduate courses in micro- and macro-economic theory and government–business relations.

While this background is impressive on some levels, it is not the sort of knowledge and experience that automatically leads to success as an entrepreneur. Being highly numerate and a great business brain are different things entirely – something Lay, Enron and the wider business world would find out soon enough.

Back then, Lay was amazed by the inefficiency of America's natural gas market. In the 1970s, US regulators did not allow interstate pipelines to pay more than 20 cents per thousand cubic feet for gas. When they were outbid by unregulated state pipelines, the regulators did not raise the maximum price threshold. Instead, they imported gas from Algeria at 10 times the domestic price. By the late 1970s, this system was on the brink of collapse, with gas shortages resulting in schools and hospitals going unheated. It did not take a PhD to spot the opportunity. Economics master Lay lobbied hard for deregulation of the market.

At the same time, he was a strong supporter of George W Bush in his efforts to become governor of Texas. When Bush was elected, Lay benefited from a law that deregulated the Texas electricity markets. Lay continued to support Bush and Cheney in their bid for the White House, becoming a so-called 'Pioneer', a supporter who collected more than US $100,000 for the campaign. He also let Bush and Cheney use his personal Enron jet to woo voters. And around the same time, during the early 1980s, he entered the world of business with the aim of capitalizing on his groundwork.

Lay took the position of president of the Continental Resources Company before joining Transco Energy Company in 1981 as president, chief operating officer and director. He joined small pipeline business Houston Natural Gas in June 1984 as chairman and chief executive officer. When it merged with Omaha-based InterNorth, Lay took the helm and the company name was changed to Enron. That was 1985.

In 1989, thanks to deregulation, Enron began to trade natural gas and the company thrived. By 1992 Enron was the largest dealer in natural gas in North America. Over the coming decade it built up a bewildering array of assets in the energy sector.

It owned a large network of natural gas pipelines that stretched across the United States, including Northern Natural Gas, Florida Gas Transmission, Transwestern Pipeline Company and a partnership in Northern Border Pipeline from Canada. It also owned pipelines in Colombia, Argentina, Bolivia and Brazil. Enron owned or operated 38 electric power plants worldwide, including in the United Kingdom, throughout Central and South America, in mainland Europe, China and India. It owned wind-generation facilities, hydroelectric and thermal plants. It also moved into paper, pulp and recycling facilities, operated a timber company in Canada and ran an oil and gas exploration, development and production business.

It is hard to say what gave Lay the confidence to diversify in this way. In November 1999 Enron launched an online trading platform called EnronOnline, enabling the company to further develop and extend its abilities to negotiate and manage its trading business. It also launched a service to enable people to trade in the United States' spare broadband capacity.

By 2001, Enron had become a conglomerate that owned and operated gas pipelines, electricity plants, pulp and paper plants, broadband assets, and water plants internationally, and traded extensively in financial markets for the same products and services.

The impact on the share price was huge: Enron's stock increased by 56 per cent in 1999 and 87 per cent in 2000. In August 2000, at the height of the dotcom boom, Enron's stock price hit an all-time high of US$90.56 and its market capitalization exceeded US$60 billion, 70 times earnings and six times book value. Enron was rated the most innovative large company in America in *Fortune*'s Most Admired Companies survey for six consecutive years, from 1996 to 2001. Yet on 2 December 2001, Enron filed for Chapter 11 bankruptcy: the biggest in US history. More than 4,000 people lost their jobs, and entire life savings went up in smoke. The stock price fell to US$0.10, losing investors something like US$11 billion.

The collapse caused the dissolution of Enron's auditors Arthur Andersen, which at the time was one of the five largest accounting firms in the world. The criminal charges that followed Enron's demise lead to the US government introducing the Sarbanes–Oxley Act in 2002, significantly raising criminal penalties for securities fraud, for destroying, altering or fabricating records in federal investigations, or any scheme or attempt to defraud shareholders.

The shame of this story is the tens of thousands of innocent men and women who were caught up in the fallout from the deceit – not only Enron employees, but those at Arthur Andersen and all those at supplier companies who relied on global behemoth Enron for their monthly pay cheque. Ken Lay went to his grave professing his innocence, blaming others, as well as the media, and talking about God. It is odd how many failed business leaders cite God in their defence. Perhaps the enormity of Lay's crimes meant that it was too much for him to bear alone. The fact that he went into business with good intentions – and did some charity work along the way – maybe led Lay to hope that he would be able to redeem himself in front of his Maker. The man was mistaken. There were early signs that Lay's management style, and his ability to hire the right people, had serious faults.

In 1987, two Enron traders got into trouble by betting on the oil markets, resulting in consistent and suspiciously high profits for Enron. The CEO of that business, Louis Borget, was also discovered to be diverting company money to personal offshore accounts. Yet Lay did not fire or discipline them. Instead, he encouraged them to 'keep making us millions', as they were making profits for the otherwise struggling company. Further bigger gambles almost cost Enron dear, and the two were finally sacked and later convicted for their crimes. Lay, meanwhile, denied having any knowledge of their activities.

In 1990, Enron hired former McKinsey consultant Jeff Skilling. During his admissions interview for Harvard Business School, he was asked if he was smart, to which he allegedly replied 'I'm f****** smart.' We shall see.

Skilling joined Enron on the condition that it begin using so-called mark-to-market accounting, allowing Enron to book potential profits on certain projects immediately after the deals were signed, whether or not those projects turned out to be successful. This gave the impression that the business was highly profitable, even if that was not true. It was a bizarre way to go about business management, and it was a decision that would prove the firm's undoing.

One of the company's biggest failures was the construction of the Dabhol Power Plant in India. Ultimately, Enron was forced to abandon the plant when it turned out that India could not afford the power Enron was producing, losing the firm US$1 billion. But using mark-to-market accounting, Enron reported profits from the Dabhol project that never arrived. Economics master Lay must have realized what was happening.

One of Skilling's favourite books at Harvard was said to be *The Selfish Gene* by Richard Dawkins, about how humanity survives by genetically passing on greedy and competitive traits. It is said that Skilling institutionalized this worldview at Enron, establishing a performance review committee that graded Enron's employees and annually fired the bottom 15 per cent, who were deemed unsuitable for the company's objectives. While charismatic, Skilling was also 'very, very intimidating', according to one former employee. 'You were certain he was just the brightest guy around, but in hindsight I really feel we were somewhat like cult followers'.

Another Enron employee who helped cause the firm's demise was chief financial officer Andrew Fastow. On 28 June 1999, Enron's board of directors exempted Fastow from the company's code of ethics so that he could run a private equity fund, called LJM1, that would raise money for and do deals with Enron. It was a tool that allowed Enron to manage its balance sheet and make investors think that it was performing better than it was. On 12 October 1999, the board again exempted Fastow from Enron's code of ethics so that he could raise money for another fund, LJM2. Fastow went on to devise all manner of off-balance-sheet schemes that hid losses in the company. It is difficult to accept that Lay was unaware of any of it.

It is yet another example of 'clever financial engineering' – a precursor to the credit crunch. In the meantime, Enron traders were working out more complex ways to make money. One of these was to manipulate the California energy market, a policy that made Enron a great deal of money but that brought rolling power blackouts to the state.

While the list of dubious employees could run and run, it is worth mentioning Lou Pai, the CEO of Enron Energy Services (EES). The Chinese-born Pai was renowned for his ruthlessness – Skilling called him 'my ICBM' (that is, an intercontinental ballistic missile). Yet Pai was also notorious for using money from Enron to feed his habit of visiting strip clubs, and for allegedly inviting strippers into his office and onto the Enron trading floor. He resigned abruptly from EES with a US$250 million pay-off, even though the divisions of Enron he formerly ran lost a total of US$1 billion. Pai later divorced his wife and married a stripper.

It is odd that Lay, this man of God, would allow this kind of behaviour from a senior executive. It seems as though the fact that Lay made a lot of money for the company got him off the hook. Is that what it taught in Lay's Bible? Throughout all these shenanigans, Lay was in charge of Enron. The idea that he did not know what was happening, that he was somehow insulated from all these major transactions, is laughable.

But while Skilling was aggressive and Pai a womanizer, it was Fastow's creative accounting methods that would ultimately bring the company down.

It was Enron insider Sherron Watkins who first noticed something was wrong with the numbers. In 1996 she was working with Fastow. 'I was starting to see Andy Fastow cross the line,' she said, claiming he asked her to lie to one of Enron's partners about an investment. 'It should have been a huge warning flag,' she says. Instead she moved to a different part of the business and became a vice president. In 2001, though, she was working for Fastow again. This time, she stumbled across evidence of massive fraud.

Watkins was looking at an Excel spreadsheet listing 200 assets that Enron wanted to sell to raise cash. Against half a dozen, she saw the name 'Raptor'. This referred to complex off-the-books partnerships used to hedge assets. 'I was seeing hundreds of millions of dollars in the loss column. I mean you couldn't do the math, it didn't work'. Watkins wrote a memo to Lay outlining her fears that Enron might 'implode in a wave of accounting scandals'. An internal investigation dismissed her claims.

Enron's dubious accounting and reporting was gaining ever more interest from financial journalists and analysts. When questioned, the top brass were aggressive, dismissive and derisory about their accusers. In fact, for any aspiring journalist, this aggressive and dismissive reaction to questioning is a sure sign something is up.

Time and time again, Lay reassured investors and employees that there were no problems. In fact, Lay regularly encouraged employees to invest in Enron stock even as it was falling from its US$90 peak – at the same time that he, his wife, and the likes of Skilling were furiously selling off millions of dollars worth of stock in secret. On 26 September 2001, Lay told Enron employees that the firm's stock is an 'incredible bargain' and that the 'third quarter is looking great'. A month later, on 16 October, Enron reported a US$618 million third-quarter loss. It was inexcusable behaviour from Lay, and it was to prove a considerable nail in the Enron coffin.

Initially when news of the accounting problems broke, Lay continued to pledge his support for Fastow, saying he had 'operated in the most ethical and appropriate manner possible'. The next day Fastow was booted out, and soon afterwards the Securities and Exchange Commission started a formal investigation.

While Lay attempted to sign a last-ditch deal with rival firm Dynergy to buy Enron, further downward restatements of earnings meant that it would never happen. On 23 January 2002, Lay resigned as chairman and CEO of Enron.

The court cases and charges soon came. Fastow was indicted on 78 charges of conspiracy, money laundering and fraud.

He was convicted and jailed for 10 years. (His wife got one year for filing a false tax report.) Skilling pleaded not guilty to wire fraud, securities fraud, conspiracy, insider trading and making false statements on financial reports. He got 24 years in prison. Various others were charged and convicted. Others committed suicide. Enron had gone from America's seventh-largest company to nothing: it was a bloody mess.

When, in 2002, the Enron issues came before a US Senate Commerce Committee, Lay, who was boldly stating he had done nothing wrong, pleaded the Fifth Amendment. He told the committee, 'I respectfully ask you not to draw a negative inference because I am asserting my Fifth Amendment constitutional protection on instruction of counsel.'

The committee was not happy. Senator Ron Wyden summed it up: 'The fact of the matter is, it's just not possible to determine why the Enron ship is at the bottom of the ocean unless you hear from the captain.' Senator Byron Dorgan added, 'The bankruptcy of this corporation is not a garden-variety business failure. It's a bankruptcy framed by very serious questions about the behavior of officers, directors and the accounting firm that audited the corporation's books.' Senator Peter Fitzgerald pitched in with 'Mr Lay, I've concluded that you're perhaps the most accomplished confidence man since Charles Ponzi.'

As it turns out, Lay's heart attack proved a financial boon for his family. With no one to pass sentence on, the charges were thrown out and the family got to keep the money they made from the fire sale of Enron stocks. The Lord does indeed work in mysterious ways.

Throughout the whole Enron saga Ken Lay was central. A friend of the Bush family (George W famously referred to him as 'Kenny boy') and a keen philanthropist, Lay was famed for 'an avuncular manner that endeared him to employees, business partners and politicians alike'. He was most often described as grandfatherly. Lay said he took responsibility for Enron's collapse, but bizarrely, denied that he had done anything wrong. 'I continue to grieve, as does my family, over the loss of the company and my failure to be able to save it,' he said. 'But failure does not equate to a crime'.

Lay added, 'I lived my life in a certain way to make sure that I would never violate any law, certainly never any criminal laws, and always maintained that most important to me was my integrity, was my character and my values.' Jurors in the trial didn't agree. They said that neither Lay nor Skilling showed much in the way of humility on the stand. Prosecutor Kathy Ruemmler agreed. She said that their 'extraordinary arrogance' is the 'exact same tactic that they used when they were running Enron' (McLean and Elkind, 2006). In the end, they were found out.

SOURCES

Allen, H (2006) Ken Lay's last evasion, *Washington Post*, 6 July

American Patriot Friends Network (nd) Enron's Kenneth Lay [online] www.apfn.org/ENRON/lay.htm (accessed 22 February 2010)

Australian Graduate School of Management (nd) Enron Timeline [online] www.agsm.edu.au/bobm/teaching/BE/Enron/timeline.html (accessed 22 February 2010)

BBC (2002a) Enron Timeline, 15 June [online] http://news.bbc.co.uk/hi/english/static/in_depth/business/2002/enron/timeline/default.stm (accessed 22 February 2010)

BBC (2002b) Andersen guilty in Enron case [online] http://news.bbc.co.uk/1/hi/business/2047122.stm (accessed 22 February 2010)

CNN Money, 18 May 2006

Crawford, K (2004) Lay surrenders to authorities, CNN Money, 12 July [online] http://money.cnn.com/2004/07/08/news/newsmakers/lay/ (accessed 22 February 2010)

Curwen, L (2003) Sherron Watkins, whistleblower, *Guardian*, 21 June

Dunn, A and Calkins, L B (2006) Enron's Kenneth Lay defended at his memorial service, Bloomberg, 12 July [online] http://www.bloomberg.com/apps/news?pid=20601103&sid=ahb42J1i1j3M&refer=us (accessed 22 February 2010)

Foley, S (2006) Kenneth Lay, obituary, *Independent*, 6 July

Guardian (2006) Timeline: Enron, 30 January [online] http://www.guardian.co.uk/business/2006/jan/30/corporatefraud.enron (accessed 22 February 2010)

Internet Movie Database (2005) 'Independent Lens': Enron: The Smartest Guys in the Room (review) www.imdb.com/title/tt0413845 (accessed 22 February 2010)

Lay, K (nd) Megatrends of energy, *World Energy Source* [online] http://www.worldenergysource.com/articles/text/lay_WE_v1n1.cfm (accessed 22 February 2010)

McLean, B and Elkind, P (2006) Enron: Some things don't change, *Fortune*, 18 May [online] http://money.cnn.com/2006/05/18/news/newsmakers/enron_blog_fortune/index.htm (accessed 22 February 2010)

Moreno, S (2006) Lay is remembered as a 'straight arrow', *Washington Post*, 13 July [online] http://www.washingtonpost.com/wp-dyn/content/article/2006/07/12/AR2006071201776_pf.html (accessed 22 February 2010)

Morgan, Dan and Behr, Peter (2002) Enron chief quits as hearings open, *Washington Post*, 24 January

New York Times, 3 May 1985

New York Times (2006) Enron Timeline, 1 February [online] http://www.nytimes.com/ref/business/20060201_ENRON_GRAPHIC.html (accessed 22 February 2010)

NNDB (nd) Ken Lay [online] http://www.nndb.com/people/974/000022908/ (accessed 22 February 2010)

Pasha, S and Seid, J (2006) Lay and Skilling's day of reckoning, *CNN Money*, 25 May [online] http://money.cnn.com/2006/05/25/news/newsmakers/enron_verdict/ (accessed 22 February 2010)

The Smartest Guys in the Room

The Times (2006) Obituary: Ken Lay, 6 July

Tolson, M (2006) Memorial service: Ken Lay praised by family and friends, 13 July [online] http://www.chron.com/disp/

story.mpl/metropolitan/4043620.html (accessed 22 February 2010)

Wikipedia (nd a) Beta Theta Pi [online] http://en.wikipedia.org/wiki/Beta_Theta_Pi (accessed 22 February 2010)

Wikipedia (nd b) Enron [online] http://en.wikipedia.org/wiki/Enron (accessed 22 February 2010)

Wikipedia (nd c) Sim Lake [online] http://en.wikipedia.org/wiki/Sim_lake (accessed 22 February 2010)

Wikipedia (nd d) The Enron scandal [online] http://en.wikipedia.org/wiki/Enron_scandal (accessed 22 February 2010)

Wikipedia (nd e) Ken Lay [online]

Chapter Fourteen

Kevin Leech
– How to Blow a Billion

Kevin Ronald Leech grew up in Manchester and left school aged 15 with eight O levels. His father ran a garage but also operated a small undertaking business. On the death of his father, aged just 51, Kevin, who had been training to become an accountant, took control of the family funeral directors. He was 21.

Leech, to his credit, built the funeral firm into a 38-strong chain of undertakers, ultimately selling it in 1982 to the Co-operative Group for around £2.5 million. Nearing the age of 40, he then upped sticks and moved to Jersey, which had better weather and a much more tax-friendly environment – and no doubt wondered what he was going to do with all that money.

It had not been an easy start in business for Leech. In order to raise the £3,000 he needed to buy out the rest of the family in the beginning, Leech had to turn to the family solicitor for a personal guarantee. 'In 1964 when I wanted help, nobody would help me,' he says.

> There were no venture capital funds then. There were no tax breaks for people. So I made a conscious decision... that I would back people when banks couldn't help. Banks can only help when you are successful. Banks can only help when you have got collateral.

With his new-found wealth, Leech set about making investments, and he soon became known as a venture capitalist. He took a punt on a Liverpudlian chemist called Jeremiah Milner who was looking for backing for his new form of kidney treatment which, he said, would improve the lives of patients, cut dialysis time and sharply reduce the risk of infection. Leech was convinced and invested £50,000 for a substantial 68 per cent stake in the company, ML Laboratories. It was a shrewd move, and proved Leech had the talent for spotting and negotiating good deals. It wouldn't always be this way.

In 1987, the Merseyside Science Park-based company became the first public biotechnology business to be listed on the London Stock Exchange. In 1991, the shares soared by 310 per cent to some £9 each, valuing Leech's stake at £170 million. A stockbroking circular at the time suggested the shares could reach £25 and that the drug could prove helpful in treating Aids. That would have meant Leech's original £50,000 investment would have become nearly £500 million.

It didn't quite work out like that, as the relationship between Leech and the widow of the founder later soured. Nevertheless, in 1996 Leech made £55 million from the sale of some of his ML Laboratories shares. And this time, he really went to town. Already a big fish in the rarefied atmosphere of Jersey, Leech had greater ambitions.

The 1990s must have felt like a heady time for Leech. In 1996, the *Independent* newspaper called him 'one of Britain's most powerful business angels', adding that he had a 'sure touch' when it came to investing. One thing that was certain was Leech's prolificacy.

Leech embarked on one of the most random acquisitions sprees the United Kingdom had ever seen. And random is the word. Like many entrepreneurs, Leech fell into the trap of believing that because he was successful in one field he could easily transfer those skills – and his acumen – to any other area of business. But while this approach may have worked for the likes of Virgin founder Richard Branson, and no doubt makes for an interesting term of study on a Harvard MBA, there is only one Branson – and business theory and business practicality do not mix. The way Branson stretched his brand is the exception that proves the rule. Leech did not even have a brand. He formed various property and leisure holdings, such as Queensborough Holdings and Heritage Great Britain, most of which were related to secretive Jersey-based trusts. To this day it is difficult to really work out exactly what he does and does not own.

At one time or another Leech's eclectic business empire included the Needles Pleasure Park on the Isle of Wight, the Cheddar Gorge Cheese Company, adventure park Lightwater Valley, the Land's End Hotel, the John O'Groats Hotel, the Snowdon Light Railway, various caravan parks and, bizarrely, the Robin Reliant car company.

It is fair to say that the Needles Pleasure Park on the Isle of Wight receives mixed reviews. While some enjoy it, others note that it is '1950s Britain at its worst'. One reviewer on tripadvisor.com comments, 'The Needles is totally spoilt by this crummy, outdated so-called pleasure park... it is a hideous blot on a beautiful landscape'. Others on the travel advice site complain that the food is poor and the prices steep.

The Snowdon Mountain Railway, which the firm runs, is described by other members of the public who have used it and commented on tripadvisor.com, as 'cramped' and 'expensive'. And it's downhill from there in terms of reviews.

The Land's End Hotel was reviewed by a mystery guest in the *Sunday Times* in August 2008, and the conclusion was stark. 'There is something mean-spirited about Land's End Hotel,' it said. 'Everything seems to come at a cost – it feels like a money-making machine.' The review, giving the hotel a paltry one out of ten, added, 'The exterior is dull, the reception was poorly run, the rooms are poky and boring, the bed was uncomfortable.'

Of course, when running consumer-facing companies, it is hard to please all the people all the time. And with technology giving people a way to vent their spleen, it is easy to pick holes. Yet the feeling remains that Leech is not an expert in everything he invests in.

The complaints are not limited to his Cornish attractions. At the other end of the land, it's just as bad. John O'Groats is famous, at least in the United Kingdom, for being the very northerly tip of Scotland. It's the place you leave from or arrive at when undertaking a charity walk, run or cycle from one end of Britain to the other. Thousands of people head there or leave from there in the quest to raise money for charity. But you certainly wouldn't go there on holiday. One of the more promising reviews calls it 'a seedy tourist trap', while it is estimated that visitors spend on average just 10 minutes at John O'Groats. That's a long way to walk – 874 miles or 1,407 km – for a 10-minute stop. The John O'Groats Hotel remains 'closed for refurbishments', as it has been for 12 years, and local people have been calling for years for something to be done about it.

Even local politicians pile in. Jamie Stone, a member of the Scottish Parliament, quoted in the *John O'Groats Journal*, said:

> For as long as I have been [a member], John O'Groats has been a glaring example of a tourism destination whose potential has never even been remotely realised because it has been crying out for investment. The continuing impasse is nothing short of a disgrace.

All in all, Leech's is not quite the impressive haul of acquisitions that it might seem on paper. But the collection certainly is odd, especially when you put it together with Leech's other interests. His Queensborough Holdings company, run with long-time business partner Stuart Sim, has been through a number of incarnations over the years, focusing on caravan parks, restaurants and hotels. In 1995 it bought Compass Leisure and Anglia Leisure, making it one of the United Kingdom's major caravan park operators. In 1998 it acquired 46 Deep Pan Pizza outlets from City Centre Restaurants for £10 million. Leech also bought Fletcher Powerboats, the biggest maker of trailer boats in Europe, from Hornby Group.

It did not stop there. Flush with cash from his ML Laboratories stock sale, in 1997 Leech splashed out on the Robin Reliant automobile company. The Robin was basically a three-wheel fibreglass van, and owners only required a motorcycle licence to drive one. It was said that the Princess Royal bought one for her estate, the Duchess of York apparently gave one to her toe-sucking boyfriend, John Bryan, and the American Embassy retained a fleet for running errands around London. Derek 'Del Boy' Trotter, hero of the BBC's hit comedy *Only Fools and Horses*, famously plied his trade in a yellow Reliant van.

Leech insisted it was a cool business decision, but it turned out he was a Reliant collector, with four vehicles of his own. He moved the firm to share a home with Fletcher International Sportboats, in Burntwood, Staffordshire, and pressed ahead with production of up to 800 cars a year. The firm ceased trading in the year 2000, but Leech remains a director of several companies that provide spares or maintenance to the vehicles.

Life was good for Leech. Most weekends he would apparently fly his family and friends back to his native Manchester in one of his two private jets, a Mitsubishi MU-2 and a Cessna 404, and would head for his box at Old Trafford to watch Manchester United play football.

But Leech was about to become a whole lot richer. The dotcom boom at the end of the 1990s was a Klondike of opportunities for investors like Leech. He jumped in with two feet, in both the United Kingdom and the United States, and starting making multiple investments in internet start-up firms. Leech became chairman of a Nasdaq-quoted company called ci4net.com Inc. It became a publicly traded entity on 20 December 1999, following the completion of a reverse merger.

Described by Leech as an 'economic network', or 'Econet', ci4net had equity interests in around 40 internet-related partner companies. It had a 50 per cent or greater interest in 34 of these companies, and held minority interests in the remainder. These companies included eight 'internet infrastructure companies, 18 business-to-business e-commerce companies, 12 business-to-consumer e-commerce companies and one incubator company'.

If Leech's pace of acquiring companies in the early 1990s had been fast, this latest spree was of another order completely. In a statement issued at the time, Leech said, 'We intend to be the leading Econet in Europe and we are confident of our ability to continue building a foundation of investments to position ourselves to achieve this goal as the European market matures'.

On 23 February 2000, ci4net acquired trrravel.com. On 1 March 2000 it acquired Systeam SpA, 'one of Italy's leading information technology system integrators, offering robust software solutions'. Six days later it acquired a majority interest in 4th Wave Technologies, 'a provider of local ISP services and content'. Then Leech really got busy! On 22 March 2000, ci4net acquired six separate businesses, according to a statement from the firm. That's six companies in a single day. It acquired a 51 per cent equity stake in Mostra Limited, 'a firm with expertise in online and offline customer acquisition and retention strategies'. It also snapped up a 50 per cent equity stake in Chorus Inc, a company with 'expertise in assisting high-growth United States-based technology companies set up European business operations'. It acquired a 25 per cent equity interest in Enteraction TV, 'a UK-based developer of broadband and interactive TV applications', as well as taking a 50 per cent stake in Businessvillages.com, which was 'developing a series of community sites targeted at professionals'.

Finally, still on 24 March, ci4net acquired 70 per cent of ICM Resource Ltd, which operates Eazyprint.com, 'Europe's first online print shop', before rounding off the day with a 2 per cent stake in Perform.com, a business that 'had developed a suite of internet-based tools to facilitate the effective management of people, projects, goals, communications, training and development'. Get that man a drink!

After all that excitement, you might imagine Leech would require a break. Yet on 1 April 2000, ci4net acquired 5 per cent of Kismet International NV, 'a leading developer of online gaming systems'. Three days later, a ci4net subsidiary acquired e-Bidding.com Inc, 'a United States-based freight and e-commerce company the assets of which included an end-to-end transaction engine for connecting carriers and shippers'. One month later, on 1 May 2000, ci4net acquired a 51 per cent equity stake in Citee BV, 'a leading systems integrator in the Netherlands employing 275 technically trained specialists'.

The company announced that revenues for the 12 months ending 31 January 2000 were US$4,409,094, although the company recorded a net loss of US$22,833,559, for the same period. Despite these numbers, Leech somehow made it to number 17 in the *Sunday Times* Rich List in the year 2000, with an estimated 'fortune' of US$1.2 billion. He was Jersey's first billionaire.

And when the dotcom bubble burst, he became the first person in Jersey to go from billionaire to bust in double-quick time. Leech had become Icarus.

In 2002, Leech was taken to court in Jersey by HSBC in an effort to recover money he owed it. At the time, HSBC said it was attempting to recover £22 million, with Leech stating his assets as being worth just £15 million. It later turned out that Leech actually owed nearer £90 million in total, with the bank owed a whopping £88 million. According to documents released the following year, Barclays International Corporate Services was also owed £1.6 million, and there was an outstanding £2.5 million allegedly owed to Burger King, the fast-food franchise that Leech brought to Jersey in 1997.

Leech was declared 'en desastre', the Jersey term for bankrupt. He took the opportunity to visit his friend Paul Davidson in Marbella. Davidson, a former plumber who is known in the City of London, not surprisingly, as 'the Plumber', is another acquisitions addict. He became notorious when he placed a £5 million spread bet on the fortunes of a tiny AIM-listed biotech company. He was later found guilty of stock market abuse by the Financial Services Authority. Davidson, for one, was full of praise for Leech despite this tricky turn of events. 'Kevin is one of the nicest people who ever walked God's earth,' Davidson said at the time. 'A very generous man, one of the greatest businessmen'. Perhaps not *the* greatest, though, eh? It was some fall from glory.

As Leech's financial problems mounted, many of his tourism-related assets were transferred to Heritage Great Britain, a company owned by Cherberry, a Jersey firm. Records at Companies House state that Leech is a beneficiary of the Jersey trust that owns Cherberry.

The complexity of his business holdings shielded Leech from too much personal pain, although of course the loss of face in a place like Jersey was no doubt tough to take. But Leech wasn't exactly left in the gutter. One of the main feelings on the island at the time was the speed that it all happened. 'I don't understand how you can lose that much money,' said one resident. But did he ever have it in the first place?

Fellow biotechnology investor Sir Christopher Evans believed it was a simple case of Leech overstretching himself. 'The portfolio was extraordinary. Hindsight is a great thing, but he fell into the entrepreneur's trap of doing too many things,' Evans said.

It wasn't just the businesses Leech did invest in that caused him grief. He also apparently turned down an opportunity to take a 25 per cent stake in CV Therapeutics for US$2 million. It went on to be worth more than US$1 billion.

Leech himself was sanguine. 'It was the sheer scale of the wipeout that affected me,' he said later.

> I'd become a venture capitalist, though I don't like the term.
> I never thought the technology stocks would get hit on both
> sides of the Atlantic like they did. My borrowings had been
> reasonable and conservative compared to the total of my
> wealth at the time… But was I caught with my pants down?
> Yes.

Leech didn't have to rough it for long, though. Within two
years he was released from his bankrupt status. It was
business as normal.

In 2006, Leech returned to the City with a stake in Accura
Pharma, a business that, among other things, hoped to 'find
medical treatment for dogs that chase their tails'. Leech
owned a 28 per cent stake through his Condor Trust – something like 30 million shares. The company went public on the
UK PLUS market, for small-cap firms, and there was heady
talk of the company being 'worth as much as £135 million'
– although the caveat was that it hadn't actually generated
any revenues to date. Despite promises that thanks to the
firm's various products, the business is 'stable, proven, and
poised for significant growth', the reality was different.
In June 2009 Accura Pharma announced that 'due to the
ongoing market conditions… it is no longer appropriate for
Accura to seek admission to AIM.' This was more bad news
for Leech.

No matter, because he was quite busy enough on several
other ventures, not least with First London Securities, an
investment business with global ambition. The business 'is a
specialist finance group with a focus on asset management,
investment banking and proprietary investing and has a
successful track record in growth investment'. It claims
to be active in the technology, healthcare and energy
sectors, and 'specialises in seed and early stage investment'.
Non-executives on the First London board included Nicholas
Chance, the former CEO of Third Mile Investment. He was
also currently private secretary to HRH Prince Michael

of Kent 'and has specialist knowledge of Russia and CIS'. Alongside him as a non-exec was Conservative MP Tim Yeo, who was chairman of the All Party Environmental Audit Select Committee of the House of Commons.

Buried on page 27 of a market admissions document is the name Kevin Leech. Through his Condor Ventures, Leech owned a 34.4 per cent stake in First London. It reported a £10 million profit in 2008, and on 1 April 2009, announced it was changing its corporate structure 'to create a new Isle of Man incorporated and tax resident holding company'.

Despite seemingly having his hands full with this, Leech has still found time to chair an online poker firm called Devilfish Gaming. It floated on the PLUS market on 5 March 2008, and Leech holds around 18 per cent through a discretionary trust called La Vignette Ventures. La Vignette, by the way, is (or was) the name of Leech's opulent Jersey home. Market documents filed in relation to Devilfish state how Leech has directorships currently with 14 companies, listing another 19 companies where he was a previous director (Devilfish, nd). Where does he get his energy?

SOURCES

Clein, D (2001) Legal deal rumours lift ML, *Liverpool Daily Post*, 8 June

Court, M (2002) Jersey officials begin to unravel Leech's assets, *The Times*, 12 October [online] 2002http://business.timesonline.co.uk/tol/business/article1169905.ece (accessed 22 February 2010)

Daily Telegraph, October 11, 2002

Devilfish (nd) www.devilfishgamingplc.com

Durman, P (2002) John o'Groats goes to Jersey, *Sunday Times*, 13 October

Durman, P (2006) Seeking a cure for what ails Fido, *Sunday Times*, 17 September

English, S (2000) Leech to contest Milner Labs writ, *Daily Telegraph*, 6 July

First London Securities (nd) www.firstlondonsecurities.com

Fletcher, R (2002) The bust billionaire Kevin Leech was once the richest man in Jersey, but the dotcom collapse has felled him, *Daily Telegraph*, 13 October [online] http://www.telegraph.co.uk/finance/4493509/The-bust-billionaire-Kevin-Leech-was-once-the-richest-man-in-Jersey-but-the-dotcom-collapse-has-felled-him.-Richard-Fletcher-describes-the-heady-flight-into-desastre.html (accessed 22 February 2010)

Foley, S (2002) Jersey courts start trawl of bankrupt tycoon's web of trusts, *Independent*, 12 October [online] http://www.independent.co.uk/news/business/news/jersey-courts-start-trawl-of-bankrupt-tycoons-web-of-trusts-613849.html (accessed 22 February 2010)

Goodman, R (2008) Devilfish Gaming is raising stakes for float, *Sunday Times*, 3 February

Grimond, M (1996) Biotech backer's new baby is caravan parks, *Independent*, 6 April

Grimond, M (1997) Queensborough in the black after 13 years, *Independent*, 5 April

Guardian, December 26, 2004

Heritage Great Britain (nd) [online] www.heritagegb.co.uk (accessed 22 February 2010)

John O'Groats Journal (date unknown) www.johnogroat-journal.co.uk

Lonely Planet

Management Today (1992) Kevin Leech's life after death, 1 February [online] http://www.managementtoday.co.uk/search/article/408941/uk-kevin-leechs-life-death/ (accessed 22 February 2010)

Manchester Evening News (2001) Cash share deal ends biotech row, 27 September

Murray-West, R (2001) Milner dispute settled at ML, *Daily Telegraph*, 28 September [online] http://www.telegraph.co.uk/finance/2735413/Milner-dispute-settled-at-ML.html (accessed 22 February 2010)

Murray-West, R (2002) Departing Leech springs bankruptcy surprise, *Daily Telegraph*,. 11 October [online] http://www.

telegraph.co.uk/finance/2829904/Departing-Leech-springs-bankruptcy-surprise.html (accessed 22 February 2010)

PR Newswire (nd) CI4net.com reports year-end results [online] www.prnewswire.co.uk/cgi/news/release?id=19928 (accessed 22 February 2010)

Real Business (2007) Seducing an angel, 30 August

Tripadvisor (nd) Reviews of Land's End Hotel, www.tripadvisor.co.uk

Sunday Times, August 23, 2008

Walsh, C (2004a) Leech's ticket to ride again, *Observer*, 15 August

Walsh, C (2004b) The fall and rise of Kevin Leech, *Observer*, 26 December

wikipedia (nd) Lightwater Valley accident [online] http://en.wikipedia.org/wiki/Lightwater_Valley#Accident (accessed 22 February 2010)

Young, R (2000) Final punchline for Reliant's three-wheel joke, *The Times*, 27 September

www.business.com

www.thisisjersey.com

Chapter Fifteen

James Cayne
– A Bridge Too Far

'James Cayne isn't one for small talk at the bridge table,' says Britain's number one player Andrew Robson. 'And after a game, you won't see too much of him. He probably won't stop by for a chat or a drink. That's not really his style. When Cayne plays bridge, he's there to win. He's fiercely competitive.' Others say that while Cayne certainly knows his spades from his diamonds, like many wealthy people on the bridge circuit, he tends to hire in top players to be part of his team, making him appear better than he actually is.

Cayne has played bridge his whole life. He moved to New York in 1969 to become a bridge professional, and has been a regular feature on the US bridge circuit, picking up a number of championship wins, both regional and national, along the way. To this day he is a regular player on online bridge websites. But it is fair to say that Cayne is not terribly popular in the world of bridge – not that he seems to care what people think of him.

On 19 July 2007, Cayne was playing in the Spingold KO bridge tournament in Nashville, Tennessee. His neuropsychologist wife Patricia, another bridge aficionado, accompanied him to the 10-day competition. Bridge is a logical game requiring the need to concentrate for long periods. With tournaments lasting weeks, and games up to 10 hours, it also needs stamina. It is a game that requires players to make fast decisions based on the information available. It is particularly popular with financiers and traders, people who are used to making quick judgment calls – people like James Cayne. It is also very addictive.

What was perhaps odd about Cayne's 2007 Nashville appearance, though, was the fact that the competition took place at a time when his company, Bear Stearns, of which he was CEO, was on the brink of collapse. While he was playing cards, back in New York two of the firm's hedge funds were in serious trouble.

Bear Stearns was finally purchased in March 2008 in an emergency rescue takeover by rival investment bank JP Morgan with the help of the US Federal Reserve. JP Morgan initially offered to buy the firm for US$236 million, or US$2 per share, but shareholder anger lead to an improved offer of US$1.1 billion, or US$10.82 per share. A year earlier, the shares had traded for more than US$170 per share. During that year, Cayne, with a 3 per cent personal stake in the business, managed to lose close to US$1 billion – a remarkable feat. Meanwhile, more than 7,500 Bear Stearns employees lost their jobs.

Bear Stearns was founded as an equity trading house in 1923 by Joseph Bear, Robert Stearns and Harold Mayer. It survived the 1929 Wall Street crash, opened a branch office in Chicago in 1933 and expanded globally, first to Amsterdam, in 1955. Headquartered in New York, it later opened offices across the United States, and throughout Europe, the Far East and China.

Over the years, Bear Stearns evolved from a company simply focused on trading securities and acting as the back office for other Wall Street firms into one with a number of interests. It served corporations, institutions, governments and individuals, and offered a range of services. These included corporate finance, mergers and acquisitions work, private client services, derivatives, foreign exchange and futures sales and trading, and asset management services. In 1985 it became a publicly traded business.

In 2005, according to *Fortune* magazine, Bear Stearns was one of the 'most admired' securities firms because of, among other things, its 'quality of risk management and business innovation'. By November 2006 the company had total capital of approximately US$66.7 billion and total assets of US$350.4 billion, making it the seventh-largest securities firm in terms of total capital. But its phenomenal growth was built on the quicksand of the US sub-prime lending market, and it would not last.

The root of the sub-prime crisis goes back years. The US Congress established Fannie Mae, or the Federal National Mortgage Association, in 1938 to make mortgages more available to low-income families. Freddie Mac, the Federal Home Loan Mortgage Corporation, was created in 1970 to expand the secondary market for mortgages in the United States. Along with other government-sponsored enterprises, Freddie Mac bought mortgages on the secondary market, pooled them, and sold them as mortgage-backed securities to investors on the open market.

With then President Clinton talking up universal home ownership, the US mortgage industry accused of 'predatory mortgage lending' and interest rates at record lows, the scene was set for financial disaster. Yet with record growth and impressive balance sheets, few stopped to complain. But in order to manage the higher risk associated with big or dubious mortgages, investment banks required a means of trading the debt on. They devised a means of pooling the loans and paying a credit rating agency to rate them. The pools formed an asset base from which they could sell bonds, which were liquid and could be traded. The complexity of these mortgage-backed financial instruments meant few of those at the top of big US institutions appeared to really understand the risks involved. If they did understand, they did not let on.

By 2007/08, Bear Stearns had notional contract amounts of approximately US$13.4 trillion in derivative financial instruments. But it had only US$11.1 billion in tangible equity capital supporting US$395 billion in assets, a leverage ratio of more than 35 to one. And that was not good, because when the whatsit hit the fan, and investors started to want their money back, it simply was not there. The inevitable happened.

They say that the young James Cayne's ideal job would have been a bookmaker. Growing up in Evanston, Illinois, he certainly was not too interested in education, dropping out of university before he graduated and 'spending more time playing bridge at his fraternity house and on intramural sports than studying'. He once explained that 'I don't read and absorb, I hear and I absorb.' His early jobs included driving a cab in Chicago, selling photocopiers and working for his father-in-law's scrap-iron business.

But backwater Illinois was not for Cayne. He headed for New York with aspirations to be a professional bridge player. He again drove a cab, sold adding machines, and worked at Lebenthal & Co selling municipal bonds. It was while in New York he met his now wife Patricia, who told him he had to get 'a proper job'. He went off to Bear Stearns.

It was 1969, and Cayne had an interview at the firm with Harold Mayer Jr, the son of one of three founders of the firm. It did not go well, by all accounts, but on the way out he spoke with Alan Greenberg, then a senior manager at the company. In an effort to make small talk, Greenberg asked Cayne if he had any hobbies. 'And I said, "Yes, I play bridge",' Cayne recalled. Greenberg, also a keen player, asked him if he was any good, to which Cayne responded, 'Mr. Greenberg, if you study bridge the rest of your life, if you play with the best partners and you achieve your potential, you will never play bridge like I play bridge'.

Greenberg was impressed, and Cayne got a job working for him in the brokerage division at Bear Stearns, catering to wealthy individuals. While there he developed a rapport with Greenberg, with the pair often playing bridge after hours at the Regency Whist Club in New York. Other players at the club included Laurence Tisch, chief executive of CBS, and Milton Petrie, chairman of Petrie Stores. There was a bridge set of people, almost Masonic in terms of their contacts and friendships. It was to become an enduring theme for Cayne.

Cayne rose through the ranks at Bear Stearns, but he really earned his stripes during New York City's 1975 financial crisis. The city was teetering on the edge of bankruptcy, and one of Cayne's clients wanted to sell some of his New York City bonds. The trouble was, no one wanted them. Cayne decided that Bear Stearns should make the market (that is, purchase the bonds itself as an interim measure), at a cost of US$5 million. While Greenberg said no, Cayne went over his head. Bear Stearns bought the bonds, and was able to find buyers for them at small brokerages around the city for prices higher than he had paid. It was quite a coup.

In 1978 Cayne joined the company's powerful executive committee, and not long after the firm went public in 1985, he became president. He became CEO in 1993, and (while continuing as CEO) chairman of the board in 2001. It was certainly a period that the business flourished: its stock price rose nearly 600 per cent. In 2006, Cayne took home US$34 million and became the first Wall Street chief to own a company stake worth more than US$1 billion. Throughout it all, Cayne played bridge.

But the richer he got, and more senior he became, the more Cayne's hands-on involvement with the firm lessened. While he was lauded by colleagues as a 'great captain' and someone good at delegating authority, the fact was that increasingly, Cayne was not in the office. During the summer, he typically left the office on Thursday afternoon, taking a 17-minute, US$1,700 trip by helicopter, to play a game of late-afternoon golf at the exclusive Hollywood Golf Club in New Jersey. He would usually play Friday and all weekend. In the evenings, he would play bridge online. The policy at the Hollywood Club is that players cannot use mobile phones or other electronic devices, although Cayne apparently used to check in with the office via the course's ninth-hole land line.

While this approach to his work was wholly acceptable during the good times, finding that Cayne was busy teeing off or playing cards when the firm began to wobble towards the brink was not. But before Bear Stearns reached crisis point, Cayne himself came close to the edge. Although it was not reported at the time, in September 2007 Cayne, then aged 73, nearly died. Rushed to hospital, he was drowsy, weak and had no appetite. Cayne insisted on being driven to hospital in a car rather than call an ambulance, fearing the impact of a public disclosure about his health on the firm. As it was, Bear Stearns was starting to feel the pinch of the markets, and a health scare to its CEO might just add to the problems.

Diagnosed with an infection in the prostate, his chances of survival were 50:50. The hospital reportedly pumped him with 22 gallons of saline and antibiotics. He was in the hospital for 10 days and shed 30 pounds. It was a close thing.

At the same time, there were increasing problems at Bear Stearns. In 2007 US home prices began to fall, and mortgage defaults were rising. In February, an index that tracked packages of sub-prime loans that had been sliced up and resold to investors in the form of complex securities started to fall. The problem for Bear Stearns was that two of its hedge funds, investment partnerships for rich people and institutions, were heavily invested in such securities. The funds used borrowed money to amplify their bets, magnifying both gains and losses. One was called the Bear Stearns High-Grade Structured Credit Strategies Fund, the other had the same name plus the words 'Enhanced Leverage'.

The bottom line was that when the market took a turn for the worse, the values of the funds dropped, meaning investors suddenly got very jumpy and started demanding their money back. The knock-on effect was that confidence in Bear Stearns started to waver. The writing was on the wall.

'Bear Stearns was the most innovative, and by innovative I mean "worst", at creating these complex instruments,' said Joseph Mason, associate professor of finance at Drexel University. 'They had a cradle to grave mortgage structure. They originated it, pooled it and sold it on'. Not only that, they managed to find increasingly innovative – or risky – methods of slicing up the worst parts of the mortgage pool and selling that on. They created a way to sell on high-risk debt, but the bubble would not last. The problem with all these complex structures was that they were designed to provide high returns. Normally the higher the risk, the higher the return, so some risk could be expected, but the methods of analysis used turned out not to reflect the risk accurately for these financial instruments.

Cayne attempted to solve the bank's liquidity problems, first by approaching a Chinese investment bank, Citic, then by approaching the likes of Bahamas-based billionaire commodities investor, Joe Lewis. Incredibly, Cayne and Lewis reportedly bonded over a shared love of gin rummy. The relationship ended up costing Lewis a staggering US$1 billion when Bear Stearns collapsed after Cayne had somehow persuaded him to make a huge investment. 'He's an adult, not a whiner,' Cayne apparently said of the way Lewis reacted.

Goodness knows how Lewis would describe the debacle. It is remarkable that a successful businessman and supposedly shrewd global investor managed to make such a catastrophic investment decision, but he is not the first person to make a mistake of that magnitude: for instance, in 1997/98, US investor George Soros lost a massive fortune investing in Russia. At this point neither Lewis nor anyone else could save Bear Stearns.

Despite the collapse and US$10-per-share deal, Cayne reportedly remained calm. And on 25 March, the day after JP Morgan revised its bid upward, he and his wife dumped their 5.66 million Bear Stearns shares, at US$10.84 each, for US$61.3 million, so at least they would not have to worry too much about the demise of the firm. They had also recently closed on the US$27.4 million purchase of two adjacent apartments on the 14th floor of the recently renovated Plaza Hotel at the corner of Fifth Avenue and 59th Street in New York. This might explain how Cayne remained calm throughout. Despite the disaster all around him, he managed to slip away with close to US$100 million net.

No wonder the general public is getting increasingly irate in the United States. In speeches leading up to Barack Obama's election to US president, he attacked the 'ethic of greed' culture in the financial services and banking industries. He pointed the finger at 'lobbyists, greedy businessmen and complacent Washington politicians'. No one, it seems, neither the business people themselves nor the politicians charged with running the country, came away from the financial disaster unscathed.

At the final Bear Stearns shareholders meeting, Cayne commandeered the microphone. 'That which doesn't kill you makes you stronger,' he said. 'And at this point we all look like Hercules. Life goes on'. He went on to complain about a 'conspiracy' of unnamed financial sharks who were responsible for the firm's downfall, adding that he hoped that the authorities would 'nail the guys who did it'. Cayne, the bespectacled CEO of Bear Stearns for the past 15 years, certainly was not accepting any blame.

In reality, Cayne's legacy is in pieces. He was one of the few very senior people at Bear Stearns not offered a position at JP Morgan Chase. Greenberg, now 80-odd, was made vice chairman emeritus at the merged firm, and got to keep 40 per cent of any trading commissions he generates. Alan Schwartz, who took over as CEO when Cayne stepped down in January, was offered a senior investment-banking post. But Cayne did not take a role.

Cayne was widely pilloried in the press, and among former Bear Stearns employees, for his bridge-playing antics at the end. While he helped create the growth and wealth of the business, he also created a huge fortune for himself. And perhaps he was insulated from the day-to-day reality of the firm's risky business ventures.

Cayne actually joined Bear Sterns in the same year, 1969, that Dick Fuld joined Lehman Brothers. While their collapsing legacy and widespread media derision may have given both men the odd sleepless night, are they destined to remain tortured souls? It is doubtful. Months later, sat in his luxury apartment with all the comforts money can buy, does Cayne look in the mirror in anguish? Did he set out to create a fantastic reputation in the investment banking community, or did he set out to make himself very rich? The smart money is on the latter. And as he said, life – and bridge playing – goes on.

SOURCES

Bawden, T (2008) James Cayne risks lawsuit as he seeks counter-offer for Bear Stearns, *The Times*, 20 March [online] http://business.timesonline.co.uk/tol/business/industry_sectors/banking_and_finance/article3587260.ece (accessed 23 February 2010)

Cohan, W D (2008) The rise and fall of Jimmy Cayne, CNN Money, 25 August [online] http://money.cnn.com/2008/07/31/magazines/fortune/rise_and_fall_Cayne_cohan.fortune/index.htm?postversion=2008080410 (accessed 23 February 2010)

Doran, J (2006) Big shot, *The Times*, 10 May [online]http://business.timesonline.co.uk/tol/business/article1069736.ece (accessed 23 February 2010)

Forbes 400 List, 2005

Fortune, 25 August 2008

Kelly, K (2007) Bear CEO's handling of crisis raises issues, *Wall St Journal*, 1 November [online]http://online.wsj.com/article/SB119387369474078336.html?mod=home_whats_news_us (accessed 23 February 2010)

Kelly, K (2008) Where in the world is Bear's Jimmy Cayne? Playing bridge, *Wall St Journal Deal Journal* [online] http://blogs.wsj.com/deals/2008/03/14/where-in-the-world-is-bears-jimmy-cayne-playing-bridge/tab/article/ (accessed 23 February 2010)

Jagger, S (2008a) Sub-prime and banking crisis: who caused this nightmare, *The Times*, 19 March [online] http://business. timesonline.co.uk/tol/business/industry_sectors/banking_ and_finance/article3579171.ece (accessed 23 February 2010)

Jagger, S (2008b) Hopes of counter bid for Bear Stearns hit by James Cayne's share sale, *The Times*, 28 March [online] http://business.timesonline.co.uk/tol/business/industry_ sectors/banking_and_finance/article3636577.ece (accessed 23 February 2010)

Smith, D (2006) Cayne loves London, *Sunday Times*, 12 March [online] http://business.timesonline.co.uk/tol/business/ markets/united_states/article740002.ece (accessed 23 February 2010)

Stiff, P (2008) Bear Stearns: timeline to disaster, *The Times*, 14 March

Thomas, L (2008a) Down $900 million or more, the chairman of Bear sells, *New York Times*, 28 March

Thomas, L (2008b) Apology is met with silence, *New York Times*, 30 May

The Times, 10 May 2006

The Times, 28 March 2008

The Times (2008) Credit crunch: timeline of events, *Times Online*, 8 August

Wikipedia (nd a) Bear Stearns [online] http://en.wikipedia.org/ wiki/Bear_Stearns (accessed 23 February 2010)

Wikipedia (nd b) James Cayne [online] http://en.wikipedia.org/ wiki/James_Cayne (accessed 23 February 2010)

American Contract Bridge League, www.acbl.org

Bear Stearns, www.bearstearns.com

CNNMoney.com, March 27, 2008

JP Morgan, www.jpmorgan.com

Purdue University, www.purdue.edu

US Federal Reserve, www.federalreserve.gov

Chapter Sixteen

Robert Tchenguiz
– Credit Crunched

In 1948, in an effort to escape persecution in Iraq, Jewish merchant Victor Kedourie Molaaem fled to Iran. Victor changed his surname to Tchenguiz (pronounced 'chen-geez'), the Persian version of Genghis, and settled in Tehran with his wealthy wife, Violet. It was here that the couple had their three children, Vincent, Robert and Lisa. Their son Robert was born on 9 September 1960.

Victor, a very traditional Middle Eastern man, was something of a natural businessman, and became involved in a variety of activities in Tehran, including buying and selling property. Remarkably, he managed to ingratiate himself with the ruling Shah and Iran's inner circle, becoming the royal jeweller and also head of the country's mint. It was some rise – and it helped set up the family for life.

It was a cosseted existence for the Tchenguiz siblings, splitting their time between ski resorts, country clubs and upmarket American schools. Robert Tchenguiz completed his education in the United States, first taking a degree in business law at the conservative Pepperdine University in Malibu, Los Angeles, followed by postgraduate studies in New York.

On the fall of the Shah in 1979, Victor was once again forced to flee, this time heading to London. Displaying an impressive degree of financial dexterity, he also managed to move the family's money out of Iran. By 1982, Robert was working as an oil trader in the World Trade Center in New York. He visited his family in London, and stayed.

It is in London that the Robert Tchenguiz story really takes off. His family and their friends were involved in property, and young Robert joined in. The Tchenguiz myth revolves around his rags-to-riches life story, but it is clear that his father's influence was key. In the beginning, Victor put up £1 million as a bank guarantee, which is a handy start in life.

Robert's first 'deal', in 1983, was the buying of a £47,000 flat in the Marble Arch area of London, which he rented out to students or tourists. It would be the start of an incredible rise. It was during the 1980s that Robert, or Robbie as he is known to his friends, started a property business with his older brother Vincent, who had studied business admin-istration in Boston, before completing an MBA in New York, and later worked for Prudential Bache in London and Shearson Lehman Brothers. Their company, Rotch, set about building a huge property portfolio, and used a funding method that would prove extremely profitable.

The pair were in essence 'buy to let' landlords, and their approach was simple: borrow money, buy a property (either residential or office space) and use the high rental income to service the debt. With London property prices heading up, they could expect to sell the property for a healthy profit.

It became a winning formula, and one that relied on one of Robbie's strengths – number crunching.

Tchenguiz said,

> People make much of my family and my background, but what they make very little of is my love and understanding of numbers. I've always taken number methodology to deals. I assess the models, calculate the risk. Same at backgammon – I assess the game, calculate the risks. Whatever I'm doing, I'm thinking numbers.

He says his passion for numbers started at school. 'I was bad at history, good at maths'. But perhaps by concentrating on the numbers, Tchenguiz was guilty of missing the bigger picture. Being good with numbers is one thing, but predicting and beating the market on an ongoing basis is something else. Tchenguiz, like many others, saw himself as a master of the universe character.

In the short to medium term, the numbers game paid off and business was brisk. At one point, Rotch had a portfolio of 600-plus buildings worth in the region of £4.5 billion. These included the main Royal Bank of Scotland office in London, the West LB headquarters and Shell-Mex House, the art deco building on the Strand in London, formerly HQ for oil firm Shell.

In 2003 the brothers set up separate investment vehicles. Vincent set up Consensus, and Robert formed R20. Robert concentrated on leisure and retail interests, while Vincent focused on residential and technology investments. Vincent continued to control Rotch.

With such a healthy array of assets, and with a track record of profitable returns, Robert Tchenguiz set his sights on ever-bigger deals, and the banks were mostly keen to help. In August 2002, R20 paid £270 million for a portfolio of five properties occupied by BT. Tchenguiz pioneered the use of large amounts of long-term securitized debts to buy tenanted and leased pubs, teaming up with German bank West LB to build Pubmaster into a 3,100-strong estate. In fact he became quite a player in the leisure industry, and R20 morphed into one of Britain's biggest landlords. It owned various pub groups, including Laurel, Slug and Lettuce, Yates, the Globe Pub Company and Kilts, a Scottish pub chain bought from Enterprise Inns for £115 million.

In 2003, Tchenguiz refinanced his property portfolio to raise £286 million so he could buy the Odeon Cinema chain, buying out West LB's 43 per cent stake. Tchenguiz and West LB also co-owned Whyte & Mackay, the whisky group, a business deal that also involved Tchenguiz's brother-in-law, South African entrepreneur Vivian Imerman. In 2005, Tchenguiz was part of a consortium that bought super-market chain Somerfield for £1.08 billion (it was later sold for a profit), while his most audacious move was an effort to control the massive Sainsbury's supermarket chain (putting in almost £400 million for a 4 per cent stake). He was at the height of his powers, yet it also spelled the beginning of the end. When deals this big go wrong, no one can sustain the losses for long.

In 2006, Tchenguiz bid to take over Mitchells & Butlers, a UK operator of managed pubs, bars and restaurants. His 550p a share offer, later increased to 575p, was rebuffed, so instead Tchenguiz built up a 16 per cent (£600 million) holding in the group. His plan for the company was simple: demerge its property assets from its pub operations and create a tax-efficient real estate investment trust in order to realize the value of property assets (worth in the region of £5 billion).

There were other investments, in a company building masts for 3G networks, in health and fitness clubs, and even in SCi Entertainment, the software company behind the hugely successful *Tomb Raider* computer games, where Tchenguiz built a 15 per cent stake. By 2007, R20 was involved in something like £10 billion worth of business.

Tchenguiz did not seem to mind what the business was, so long as there was a return on the investment. 'I've yet to see another business like R20,' commented someone close to R20. 'It participates in private equity, buys equity and runs businesses'. The name of the game was 'extracting value'. And Tchenguiz knew his place. 'We're expected to be operators but that's not what we do,' he told *Management Today* magazine in January 2007.

> We're not operators. We tend to find appropriate operators to work for us. We don't interfere. We choose a manager and let him run it – if he's not good enough, we change him. I'm not a retailer, but I know where to go to get retail skills. I'm not a publican, but I know where to go to get publican skills. Anyone who says they have all those skills is lying.

Entrepreneurs certainly talk a good game. Many are quoted in business magazines talking sense and being successful. So why would anyone doubt them? Yet here is Tchenguiz admitting that he does not really understand the various sectors in which he is operating – any of which would take years to really understand. He is pouring the money in and relying on others to call it for him. It is a dangerous policy. In boom times, predicting ever-rising returns is simple. Understanding market forces, watching the trends: anyone can do it while the market is rising. But the boom times did not last.

The deal-making led to reams of positive press coverage for Tchenguiz. A March 2007 *Guardian* newspaper profile lauded him for his business strategy. The 'flamboyant' entrepreneur, it said, 'is an A-list dealmaker', before adding 'history has shown that he can multi-task'. It said, 'Tchenguiz has mastered the financial pyrotechnics that use vast amounts of debt to buy buildings. He wrings out extra cash, using devices such as securitisation – borrowing money against a property's future earnings.' One of the best bits, the coverage agreed, was that the R20 business was run on a relatively tiny staff of 40 people, mostly former bankers. They seemed like safe hands.

The wealth, and his increasing business profile, meant that Robbie was never far from society gossip columns. Friends included easyJet founder Stelios Haji-Ioannou, Formula One owner Bernie Ecclestone and retail entrepreneur Philip Green. There were tales of Tchenguiz being the man who introduced Diana, Princess of Wales to Dodi Fayed while staying on Richard Branson's Caribbean hideaway, Necker Island. In 2007, Tchenguiz was among the guests for Sir Philip Green's five-day 55th birthday bash in the Maldives, 'partying with superstars such as Jennifer Lopez'.

Lisa Tchenguiz, Robbie and Vincent's sister, was also in on the family fun. Today she goes by the title of executive producer, usually a film world colloquialism for being the money behind a project. She has two films to her name, *The World Unseen*, 'a story of forbidden love – both inter-racial and lesbian' and *I Can't Think Straight*, 'a light-hearted romantic comedy about a lesbian love affair between an aristocratic Arab girl and her best friend, a British Muslim'. Her first marriage, to perma-tanned DJ Gary Davies, ended in 2001. Her second, to Vivian Imerman, did not do too well either.

Robert claimed to seek a low profile, but dating the likes of former Wonderbra model Caprice did not help. He certainly enjoyed his wealth. He is a fan of fast cars, has a yacht moored in Monaco, takes part in many country shoots, and spent a cool £30 million on his house next to the Royal Albert Hall in London. For his 40th birthday party, Tchenguiz shelled out £100,000 on a Louis XVI-themed bash, complete with fire-eaters, staff in liveried costumes and wigs, a nine-piece ensemble and acrobats from the Cirque Du Soleil –very low-key.

His gossip column days are mostly behind him now, though, since he has become teetotal, married Heather Bird, and had a daughter, Violet. Bird, a US-born blonde, runs a chain of botox clinics in London. The perfectly crafted Bird prefers to be known as an 'anti-ageing visionary' according to her personal website, which includes the rather modest strapline, 'Working for a better future in a better world'. In the 'in the news' section of her website, between pieces about the miraculous treatments her firm offers, is a 2007 *Sunday Times* Rich List article (complete with picture of the grinning, shapely Bird) on hubby Robert and brother-in-law Vincent – the two being worth, at the time, £850 million.

Life was good, but it was about to go bad. Tchenguiz was mostly in the headlines for all the right reasons (Caprice aside). He was tenacious and ambitious, and his property empire was the result of astute planning and careful calculation. But one deal, in 2003, raised questions in the media – about Tchenguiz and his father, Victor.

By now Victor had moved again, this time to Israel, but he was still very much involved in a variety of business activities, including investment vehicle Aceville Investments. In 2003, Robert was planning another audacious bid (worth around £600 million), for upmarket department store Selfridges. Only it came to light that Aceville Investments was trading in Selfridges shares around the same time, causing the Financial Services Authority (FSA) and the Takeover Panel to examine exactly what was going on.

Victor Tchenguiz claimed he had not informed his son, or Lehman Brothers, the investment bank advising on Robert's potential bid, that he had been dealing in contracts for differences involving Selfridges shares. Cantor Fitzgerald, the broking firm through which Aceville bought the contracts for differences, admitted that it had 'made an internal error' by failing to disclose that Victor Tchenguiz's company had an interest in the shares. There was no action from the FSA. As it turned out, Tchenguiz lost out on the bid to Canadian billionaire Galen Weston, but the incident shone a light on to the business dealings of the brothers.

Between them, Vincent and Robert were directors of more than 300 companies each. Top of the pile was their Mayfair-based Rotch Property Group. Its biggest shareholder was a Panamanian company called Vin-Rotch Properties, and the ultimate controlling party was and is the Tchenguiz Family Trust. In fact, the brothers controlled a number of family trusts based in the British Virgin Islands and Cayman Islands.

It also came to light that the same City institutions were involved in the brothers' deals, particularly Lehman Brothers, the Royal Bank of Scotland, West LB and Icelandic bank Kaupthing. It is not so unusual for a businessman to turn to friendly banking faces when doing deals, and these deals had been profitable, but the particular banks they worked with, like Tchenguiz, were about to encounter severe financial problems.

It was not just the impending credit crunch that would cause Tchenguiz grief, though. His losses on other big deals also contributed to the feeling that he was losing his Midas touch. He borrowed heavily to accumulate his 10 per cent stake in Sainsbury's, ahead of an anticipated £10 billion buy-out by a Qatari investment fund. But the deal never happened, the shares went into freefall, and Tchenguiz reportedly lost something like £300–400 million.

It was a similar tale at SCi Entertainment. Tchenguiz took a 15 per cent stake ahead of an expected takeover but that did not happen either, leading the shares to fall some 80 per cent. Tchenguiz lost another small fortune on his Mitchells & Butlers deal as a result of a write-down following a disastrous interest-rate gamble. Any one of these would have caused Tchenguiz headaches, and put together, they spelled big trouble.

He also faced personal problems with his (by now) former business partner at Whyte & Mackay, Vivian Imerman. Imerman was splitting up with his wife Lisa (Robert's sister), and things got acrimonious, fast. An argument over the ownership of a bullet-proof Rolls-Royce led Robert to bar Imerman from their Mayfair offices. Quite why either of them required a bullet-proof car remains unclear. Imerman had to get an emergency High Court injunction to enter the Leconfield House offices and retrieve his belongings.

Back on the business front, though, Tchenguiz was about to face the greatest test of his number-crunching prowess. When both Lehman Brothers and Iceland's largest bank, Kaupthing, collapsed, Tchenguiz was exposed like never before. At one point in 2008, it is reported, Kaupthing's loans to Tchenguiz companies were equivalent to around 46 per cent of deposits held by the bank. Following the bank's implosion, regulators acting on behalf of creditors set about calling in loans and seizing assets, including a British Virgin Islands-registered holding company, Oscatello Investments.

Oscatello was originally set up by the Tchenguiz Discretionary Trust, of which Robert Tchenguiz is a beneficiary. Most of the Kaupthing loans secured by Tchenguiz were held in this holding company. In February 2009 a court filing indicated that Oscatello, then owned by Kaupthing, still owed £644 million. With the control of Oscatello, however, came ownership of interests in a number of equity investments, such as Sainsbury's and pub operator M&B.

Kaupthing, desperate, began a fire-sale of investments which included forcing through the sale of a 22 per cent stake in M&B to Joe Lewis, the Bahamas-based billionaire, much to the fury of Tchenguiz. Intriguingly, press coverage prior to the fire sale to Lewis made him out to be a benign investor, merely willing to help out Tchenguiz. It did not turn out that way.

To complicate matters further, regulators uncovered the extent to which Kaupthing and Tchenguiz were involved. Tchenguiz was not just Kaupthing's largest customer but had also led a series of private equity-style joint-venture deals in which Kaupthing had co-invested its own money.

In 2007 Tchenguiz had become a major investor and board member in Exista, an Icelandic holding company that was the largest shareholder in Kaupthing.

Compounding his woes, in 2009 Tchenguiz was hit with a £180 million lawsuit after preventing Kaupthing from seizing control of its proceeds from the sale of Somerfield. The claim includes details of a complex web of loans, shareholdings, profit participation agreements and collateral pledges between companies registered in the British Virgin Islands, the Isle of Man and Guernsey. The case rumbles on.

Could these deals have been so complicated that the entre-preneurs and businessmen who set them up did not quite understand who owed whom what? Did they foresee and plan against the failure of such a large business partner such as Kaupthing? Plainly not. In total, it was estimated that Kaupthing extended loans of £900 million to offshore firms controlled by the Tchenguiz Discretionary Trust.You do not need to be a maths expert to do the sums.

As a businessman, Tchenguiz divides opinion. One business leader called him 'a chancer, a number-crunching opportunist, who regards whichever business he happens to be investing in as a mere commodity'. Another foe is quoted as saying, 'Robbie hasn't lost three quarters of his wealth. He has lost one and a half times his wealth – because he was never quite as rich as he thought he was.' Then others say he's a 'fantastic guy to be with and more generous than anyone'. It maybe depends whether you're working with him, or negotiating against him.

Tchenguiz himself was once quoted as saying it was best not to cross him. 'They only f**k me once,' he said.

In 2008, a senior manager at Tchenguiz's R20 business was asked about the prospects for the investments in which it was active. 'It's tough to go wrong in this market,' he said, rather idiotically, as it turns out. Exactly what impact this catastrophic business storm has wreaked on Tchenguiz is unclear. He has said that he has no need to sell his Monaco-based yacht, and he still enjoys shooting trips to Waddesdon, Jacob Rothschild's estate in Buckinghamshire, so it cannot be all bad. 'I've lost a lot of money but I'm not in trouble,' Tchenguiz told one interviewer in 2009, estimating that he had lost close to £1 billion. 'It's just taking the rough with the smooth.'

Whatever the actual truth of the number and size of his losses, they are huge by any standards. But Tchenguiz may well return, bigger and better than ever – and why not? If so he might want to think about changing the family name again: to Phoenix.

SOURCES

Blackhurst, C (2007) The *MT* interview: Robert Tchenguiz, *Management Today*, 11 January [online] http://www.managementtoday.co.uk/

search/article/561465/the-imt-i-interview-robert-tchenguiz/ (accessed 23 February 2010)

Blackhurst, C (2009) City interview: Robert Tchenguiz, *London Evening Standard*, 6 March

Blitz, R (2009) Changing relationship with Tchenguiz, *Financial Times*, 5 June

Bowers, S (2009a) Tchenguiz's Icelandic saga with a bitter ending, *Observer*, 12 April

Bowers, S (2009b) Tchenguiz trust hit with £180m lawsuit, *Observer*, 17 May [online] http://www.guardian.co.uk/business/2009/may/17/somerfield-kaupthing-supermarkets-banking (accessed 23 February 2010)

Charity, P (2009) M&B gives Joe Lewis seat on board, *Morning Advertiser*, 16 July [online] http://www.morningadvertiser.co.uk/news.ma/article/83741?Ntt=joe%2Blewis%2BM%2526B&Ntk=All&PagingData=Po_0~Ps_10~Psd_Asc (accessed 23 February 2010)

Daily Telegraph, 16 July 2009

Danaher, T (2003) Tchenguiz brothers reorganise Rotch, *Property Week*, 21 March

Davey, J and Butler, S (2003) Selfridges tradesface inquiry, *The Times*, 20 May [online] http://business.timesonline.co.uk/tol/business/article1134157.ece (accessed 23 February 2010)

Guardian, 7 February 2009

Hipwell, D (2009) Icelandic authorities take ex-Tchenguiz firm to court, *Property Week*, 17 April [online] http://www.allbusiness.com/company-activities-management/company-structures/12451308-1.html (accessed 23 February 2010)

Independent, 30 January 2008

Milmo, C (2008) Crash landing: the fall of Robert Tchenguiz, *Independent*, 30 January [online] (accessed 23 February 2010)

Money Week (2007) Robert Tchenguiz defiant despite £200m Sainsbury's hit, 20 November [online] http://www.moneyweek.com/news-and-charts/robert-tchenguiz-defiant-despite-200m-sainsburys-hit.aspx (accessed 23 February 2010)

Observer, 12 April 2009

Power, H and Fletcher, R (2008) Robert Tchenguiz dismisses circling traders, *Daily Telegraph*, 3 February [online]

http://www.telegraph.co.uk/finance/newsbysector/
constructionandproperty/2783774/Robert-Tchenguiz-
dismisses-circling-traders.html (accessed 23 February 2010)

Rotch Property Group, www.rotch.com

Simpkins, E (2003) Tchenguiz paves way for Odeon bid, *Daily Telegraph*, 23 November [online] http://www.telegraph.co.uk/finance/2869777/Tchenguiz-paves-way-for-Odeon-bid.html (accessed 23 February 2010)

The Times, 17 May 2007

Trefgame, G and Keers, T (2003) Tchenguiz desire for Selfridges unshaken by probe, *Daily Telegraph*, 21May [online] http://www.telegraph.co.uk/finance/2852557/Tchenguiz-desire-for-Selfridges-unshaken-by-probe.html (accessed 23 February 2010)

Walsh, D and Power, H (2008) Robert Tchenguiz could lose up to £1bn, *The Times*, 8 October [online] http://business.timesonline.co.uk/tol/business/industry_sectors/banking_and_finance/article4909993.ece (accessed 23 February 2010)

Wood, Z (2007) Dealmaker fancies a Sainsbury takeaway, *Guardian*, 25 March [online] http://www.guardian.co.uk/business/2007/mar/25/theobserver.observerbusiness4 (accessed 23 February 2010)

Consensus Business Group, www.cbg.uk.com

http://new.u.tv, 17 May 2009

R20, www.r20.co.uk

Conclusion

Prison accounted for six of the people in this book at one time or another, one died before his trial, two committed suicide, and the rest retreated to lick their wounds. The actual combined wealth lost – or blown – is impossible to calculate.

When Lehman Brothers, led by Dick Fuld, filed for Chapter 11 bankruptcy protection, it alone cited bank debt of US$613 billion, with another US$155 billion in bond debt. Many argued that this corporate collapse in part led to the hastening of the ongoing global credit crunch. According to the International Monetary Fund, the total cost of the banking crisis was around US$11.9 trillion – or equivalent to handing out £1,779 (US$2,929) to every man, woman and child on the planet.

Robert Tchenguiz lost a combined cash and paper fortune that he estimated to be around £1 billion, while German industrialist Adolf Merckle single-handedly bet and lost several billions, much of it in cash.

Money aside, the impact of these losses was devastating. Lehman Brothers was accused of triggering the global credit crisis, no less. Bear Stearns, Enron and WorldCom managed to explode so spectacularly that they helped to destroy many thousands of jobs – not just direct employees but their suppliers, clients and their families also felt the pain. At the heart of it all were individual men – driven, ambitious and hard working no doubt, but also variously vain, greedy and egotistical as well.

The people in the book are not, in themselves, especially remarkable people. They achieved great success in many cases, but none are superhuman. In fact all of them were brought low by very human characteristics – to err is human, after all – but it does not have to be that way. Mistakes like the ones they made can be avoided, the entrepreneur's foibles spotted and handled. If not, beware.

One thing is certain: the businessmen and entrepreneurs featured here were, or are, very much 'big picture' people. They did not particularly like getting involved with the detail of their businesses. They tended to delegate to the wrong people, or if they delegated to good people, they ignored their advice. That is a recipe for disaster.

Naggar and Klimt were constantly focused on the next big deal, the next revenue stream. Tchenguiz, the property magnate, is another concerned with making another, bigger and better deal. Reuben Singh was again looking ahead, on creating another great new business, in the meantime forgetting about the day-to-day mundanity of his current business operations.

The great businesses of the 21st century do understand the detail. The managers of the likes of supermarket chains Wal-Mart and Tesco, and companies such as General Electric, Coca-Cola and HSBC, are all completely consumed with the finer details of their businesses – and doing what their customers want. They understand that the little things are important, and they know what irritates or pleases their customers. They are immersed in the detail, the nuisances and the day-to-day rigour, grind and mundanity that is their business. Because mundane is important; ordinary people understand mundane.

We live in an age where we are fortunate that we can be bored. We do not in the main, in the West, have to worry about food, shelter, political freedom or other forms of persecution. As a result, people worry about their lives and the small things that make their lives tick: their Facebook photo; what additives are in the food they are eating for breakfast; what children will be eating or drinking today. Many great businesses are built on these petty likes, dislikes and foibles. While many entrepreneurs understand this at the outset, some lose a grip on reality by the end.

Gradually, these entrepreneurs' and business leaders' attention turns towards a who-has-the-biggest-boat competition, an ever-growing property empire, a prettier girlfriend. They end up consumed by their own important lives; they lose the passion they once had for the mundane aspects of their customers' lives. With that forgotten, they run the risk of losing once loyal customers. And with that goes their business.

Money, wealth, business and material success do not equate to intelligence, yet it is surprising how many entrepreneurs think they do. It is not that successful business people are not clever, because they certainly are, but they are not necessarily *that* smart. They may have great ideas, a fabulous vision and gritted determination. They might not take no for an answer; they are resourceful, interesting, adaptable and creative. But we should not confuse this with being the smartest person in town.

Victor Kiam shot to prominence as the man who supposedly liked the Remington razor so much he bought the company. It made for a terrific ad slogan – and it worked. But it did not make Victor Kiam a world thinker.

The richest businessmen and women in the world are not the world's most intelligent or capable people. Yet is it surprising how many successful entrepreneurs disagree. Many believe that the size of their wealth, bank account and assets is directly proportional to the quality of their grey matter. It is not.

A great example is Hungarian-born George Soros: speculator, investor, gambler, benevolent philanthropist, call him what you will. Worth something like US$11 billion, his wealth is based on calling the market correctly and taking advantage of currency swings and the now much-maligned hedging. In September 1992, Soros made around US$1.1 billion when his investment fund sold short more than US$10 billion worth of British pounds, profiting from the Bank of England's reluctance to either raise its interest rates to levels comparable with those of other European Exchange Rate Mechanism countries or float the currency. Soros was called 'the man who broke the Bank of England'. Recently he has churned out a series of books putting down his various theories. Clearly the man, like many before him, wants to leave a legacy. Yet he does not want to be remembered for the way he came to have such riches, by opportunism and shrewd trading. All his interviews and PR spreads are on his ideas about capitalism, the inadequacies of the markets and the impending doom that is consequent to these failings. He wants to be remembered as an intellectual great.

Many of the people profiled here are in their 50s, 60s, 70s or more. In other words, they are old. What defines a great entrepreneur is their ability to move with the latest whims or needs of their customers and clients. New product development has never been better exemplified than by Apple Computers, with its Apple Mac, iPod, iPhone and now iPad. Apple boss Steve Jobs has to date come across much like his products – perennially hip, cool and state-of-the-art. The same cannot be said for the likes of Ken Lay at Enron, Hank Greenberg at US insurance giant AIG, or Boris Berezovsky.

The fact is that they had trouble adjusting to new thinking and changing business paradigms. What worked for Adolf Merckle for 40 years stopped working for him in 2008, and he could not comprehend why. He was emotional and hurt when people started comparing his way of conducting business with that of hedge fund traders.

Compare these approaches with the likes of US investor Warren Buffett and Australian-born news magnate Rupert Murdoch: both are cracking on in age but both are definitely moving with the times.

Watching Cristiano Ronaldo, Real Madrid's £80 million football star, speed towards defenders, stepping over the ball and twisting one way and then another, it is hard to know what is going through his mind. The guy is poetry in motion, an incredible talent, a genius. The same goes for Roger Federer and for great writers and composers. Their talent inspires awe. It is so difficult to replicate. Mere mortals understand that they can not run at pace with a ball at their feet (or at all!), or strike a cross-court smash winner. It is difficult to break down exactly what it is about these brilliant sportsmen that sets them apart, and the same can go for successful entrepreneurs. They are more than the sum of their parts. Maybe you cannot be taught what they know, but you can learn from the mistakes of others and ensure you do not repeat them. And the mistakes are often remarkably similar, and painfully human.

LESSONS IN ENTREPRENEURSHIP

Take your own advice, but do not believe your own hype

The characters in this book are full of wise advice about business and entrepreneurship, yet it is advice they rarely appeared to take themselves. Property dealer Peter Klimt told one interviewer, 'You have to create an infrastructure. Without that, what you're doing is just a series of deals, a sequence of events – not creating a business.' He did not create a sufficient infrastructure, and his business collapsed.

Another property tycoon, Robert Tchenguiz, explained, 'I've always taken number methodology to deals. I assess the models, calculate the risk.' Since he lost a billion-pound fortune, it seems he did not do enough calculating. Then there is Reuben Singh, Manchester entrepreneur and a man with a business soundbite. 'You'll never throw a six if you don't roll the dice,' he once said. Singh certainly rolled the dice – and he lost, big time.

Singh is a great example of someone who most definitely did believe his own PR. He used it to good effect as well, decorating his office with press cuttings that enabled him to secure a £1 million bank loan. Singh was once labelled a 'business hero' and even the 'British Bill Gates'. It is hard not to let that sort of thing go to your head.

Corporate leaders were just as culpable. President Bill Clinton once called Bernie Ebbers 'the symbol of 21st century America', although there may be some hidden truth in that. Jón Ásgeir Jóhannesson, the Icelandic retail tycoon, was regularly lauded for his daring business approach and 'rock star looks', while nearly all the others featured in these pages were the recipients of awards and prizes, if not for business prowess or personal achievement, then for

– rather more embarrassingly – corporate governance. The media could not have got it more wrong.

The media is a fickle mistress. That much is well known, but time and time again entrepreneurs and business leaders are drawn towards the flame of publicity. Whether it is ego, pride, part of the corporate public relations plan or just something to show their mothers, the fact is that if you are up to no good, and you are in the public eye, the media will one day come knocking – and no amount of 'no comments' or legal threats will save your skin.

Do not take revenge on your past

Not being comfortable in their skin has been a motivator for artists, composers, writers and entertainers through the ages. The likes of Picasso, Van Gogh and Leonard Cohen have all done some of their best work in the midst of despair. Harry Potter author JK Rowling, once a hard-pressed single parent, was faced with the death of her mother when she was writing the first book in the amazingly successful series.

Tough beginnings can break, but also occasionally make a person. It can be a wonderful driving force for an entrepreneur.

James Cayne of Bear Stearns was a taxi driver before joining the New York firm, where he could use his bridge skills to good effect. Bernie Ebbers ran a hotel but had dreams of greater things. Christopher Foster, the British entrepreneur, was brought up on a housing estate in Wolverhampton and started out as a salesman – but he was not finished there. He wanted to be a country gent. Robert Tchenguiz wanted to break free from his brother Vincent, and escape the label of only making it thanks to his father's money. Boris Berezovsky, the maths expert, clearly thought he was more intelligent than Russian President Putin. Reuben Singh revelled in being treated as a business celebrity, capable at a very young age of influencing senior politicians.

One thing most of those in this book have in common is something of a chip on their shoulder about who and what they are, and where they came from. Yet while proving themselves can be the motivational force that pushes them to succeed, at one point someone needs to put an arm around their shoulder and say, 'It's over, you've won. Stop fighting to prove yourself.'

Without putting a brake on themselves they risk pushing on and on, to ever greater heights, with ever-growing risks. And, like many in this book, they risk losing it all.

Accept that luck played a part in your success

Tom Wolfe's 1987 novel *The Bonfire of the Vanities* centres on Sherman McCoy, a white, multi-millionaire, New York City bond trader. He regards himself on Wall Street as a 'Master of the Universe', but succumbs to an altogether more human end. Despite the credit crunch, banking collapse and corporate bailout of 2008/09, it seems that the Master of the Universe attitude remains pervasive.

It is an attitude that is encouraged in many societies from an early age – that you can achieve anything you want, and that you too can be a millionaire. This is, after all, the American dream. But these days it is more than just Americans who share that dream. Indians, Brazilians, Russians and Chinese all want a piece of the action, and why not?

If it gives people hope and a chance, it should be encouraged.

But if you attain that wealth, if you are one of the few, you should not fall into the trap of believing that it was

somehow preordained, that it is solely down to your abilities and skills, or that your sheer brilliance is the one and
only cause. Many in this book, whether from council estates
or wealthy parentage, appear to believe that it is they and
only they who are responsible for their elevated place in
society. Yet the greatest entrepreneurs remain humble.
Richard Branson, Bill Gates and Stelios Haji-Ioannou, like
many others, put their success down to at least some luck.

Enjoy your success!

Oddly, a lot of the entrepreneurs featuring in this book did
not appear to be satisfied with their lot. They maybe owned
one antique gun to show off to fellow gun club chums, but
they wanted another. They had a penthouse in Manhattan
but it could have been bigger. They drove an expensive fast
car, but there was always another, newer, faster car hot off
the production line.

It is thoughts like these that made rational men make
irrational decisions. Particularly for those entrepreneurs
from humble roots, the excess and greed seem completely
obscene. Yes, it is right to enjoy the fruits of your labour, but
to yearn after a bigger yacht or fancier house – well, there's
always someone better off.

Being an entrepreneur is about innovating and pioneering,
yet so many fail to adapt to their new-found wealth and
circumstances. While their products may innovate, their
mentality remains locked in the past. It is a dangerous
combination.

Some of people who appear in this book, driven half mad
with ambition, fear the fall back down to the life they
thought they had left behind. But this kind of ambition can
end up with their doing just that. If only they had taken a

few deep breaths, taken some time out, maybe they would still be alive (and not in prison) today.

Unassailable wealth is a myth

The credit crunch and economic meltdown that struck the world's economies from 2007 onwards showed how even billionaires can blow it all. Many of those who built their empires on the back of property, such as Naggar, found that actually it was built on the quicksand of debt. Firms like Lehman Brothers and Bear Stearns were also caught out, not only by the insane complexity of their operations but because there was an underlying, and rather unsavoury, greed factor. Enough was not enough.

And both Lehman Brothers and Bear Stearns, with their global operations and giant office buildings staffed full of supposedly bright people, did not see it coming. Dick Fuld at Lehman Brothers, speaking to a US House Committee after the collapse of the 158-year-old investment house, told the panel that his actions had been 'prudent and appropriate'. Cayne, speaking via a microphone to crestfallen Bear Stearns executives after the firm's demise, told them, 'That which doesn't kill you makes you stronger.' Walking away with a huge payoff certainly cushioned the blow for Cayne. He added that he hoped the authorities would 'nail the guys who did it'.

Both appeared dumbstruck, in denial. That such huge institutions with such supposed wealth and power could crumble on their watch – how could it be? There was no safety in big numbers. They were not unassailable.

Some have drawn the conclusion from the credit crisis that it is a result of unrestrained capitalism. Yet such widespread and indiscriminate economic woe surely points to the fact that capitalism does a pretty decent job at pruning itself.

Not only is the 'man in the street' suffering, everybody suffers. And the destruction of wealth, both new and old money, can only be a good thing. It teaches salutary lessons for all – and yet there are specific lessons for entrepreneurs. Beware the prospect of losing it all.

Believe in the miracle of the mundane

Hundreds of small details make for a successful business. Often, these details are not incredibly exciting. Even more often, they are not particularly intellectually stimulating or the least bit interesting. And they are not funny either. But the detail is critical, perhaps the most critical aspect of the entire business. So do not forget it.

Those people looking for the meaning of life in business should end their search and start studying philosophy. Those wanting to marvel at the beauty and functioning interactivity of people working together as a coherent team pursing goals and objectives should continue to run their successful businesses.

Many of the entrepreneurs and business leaders in this book appear to have forgotten how incredible they were as human beings – and how unbelievably lucky they have been as individuals. Yet instead of enjoying the game of life, the score became the only important thing. Most of those in this book seem to have felt they had become too important to get involved in the detail, or too grand to keep a grip on what they knew or what their original business model was. And when they became too important to talk to customers, or to find out what their staff were feeling about the path they are following, they were doomed.

If you do not understand something, others will mislead you

A lot of problems start for entrepreneurs and business leaders when their business becomes too complicated. It gets to the stage when they do not really know what is going on – and that is deadly. In most situations, it is a case of hiring a trusted lieutenant or relying on a series of highly qualified people to understand it for you.

It is not that Steve Jobs at Apple or Larry Ellison at Oracle have to understand what their programmers are doing every day, but they do need to be aware of the business model, and they are. They know and understand how they are making money, what is important to customers and what their clients want. It is hard to say the same for Bear Stearns and Lehman Brothers. In Jón Ásgeir Jóhannesson's case, did he really understand the financial engineering behind the deals he was doing? Did he understand the risks? If he did not, he should have. If he did, he was bordering in the insane.

Ken Lay was undoubtedly a smart guy, but did he rely too much on people who said they knew what was going on when they clearly did not? The evidence would point to a big fat yes.

Jeff Skilling famously said he was 'f****** smart'. And we all know what happened to him: he is currently a prisoner and resides behind bars in Colorado.

The problem with trusted lieutenants, often, is that they will tell you what you want to hear. And when the poop hits the fan they will simply lie to you. It is better all round for you to understand your own business.

Does your business make realizable profits?

It is all very well being worth a billion dollars on paper. It may well open doors for you, mean you can afford a big house, fancy car, and join the highly prestigious golf or bridge club, but without real profits, the business is built on nothing. And while this might be sustainable short term, the credit crunch and economic meltdown globally has shown that it is not a very clever long-term position, even for the high and mighty like Lehman Brothers and Bear Stearns.

What these and other firms have relied on, so-called 'clever' financial engineering, is at the root of the global credit crisis. The problem is that the complexity of their businesses meant no one at the top really understood what was going on or the level of the risks. Or if they did, they were suicidal.

Luke Johnson, the British serial entrepreneur and venture capitalist, draws a clear distinction between entrepreneurs and the so-called 'geniuses' running the banks. Writing in the *Financial Times*, he said the difference between them is that entrepreneurs 'rely on hard-won trial and error, gut instinct and a need to really know what they are doing'. The bankers, on the other hand, relied too much on 'arcane spreadsheets and too much financial engineering'. He continued, 'These "masters of the universe" did not have enough to lose personally.'

It is a similar story to the demise of British bank Barings. Complex derivatives trading by trader Nick Leeson brought it down. The management was not aware of what he was doing, and the hole into which Leeson was digging the business.

The same attitude to risk was evident in the cases of Icelandic retailing tycoon Jón Ásgeir Jóhannesson and British property magnate Robert Tchenguiz. Actually the pair were interlinked, via Icelandic bank Kaupthing, and suffered an agonizing death waltz together as the world woke up to the insanity of Iceland's supposed place at the top table of international banking. Here was a country of 300,000 people, governed and ruled by a tiny elite, who managed to convince themselves and the rest of the world that they were 'the real deal' – an economic force. It was unbelievable because it was not true. No one listened and no one cared because of the massive fees attached to the deals.

Once entrepreneurs become so far removed from their business that they no longer understand how it makes money, they had better hope they have turned over responsibility of running it day-to-day to someone who does. If not, expect to be featured in the next edition of this book.

One more deal will not salvage a broken business model

In 1999, Bernie Ebbers announced that MCI WorldCom would attempt to acquire its rival Sprint Communications for $115 billion. In August 2008, British insulation entrepreneur Christopher Foster was talking about signing a massive deal with Russian businessmen that would take his business into another stratosphere. Neither of the deals happened. WorldCom collapsed and Ebbers ended up in prison. Foster took his own life.

It is incredible how many of the entrepreneurs in this book attempted to pull off the most audacious deals of their lives just as their firms were teetering on the brink of collapse, as if there was a magic bullet solution, as if what had worked before would work again. But it would not. Things had moved on. Time had caught up with them, and by then it was too late. In all cases, if they had slowed down sooner, had better advice or concentrated on the business in hand rather than on the never-ending quest for business conquests, some of those featured here would not be.

Legacy: follow Gates and Carnegie

No one will speak in hushed tones about the flash cars driven around the streets of Shanghai by Chinese entrepreneur Zhou Zhengyi in years to come. Luxury ski chalets or sun-drenched Caribbean hideaways are not the stuff of legacies. Yet many of these entrepreneurs are desperate to be remembered, to leave a legacy, to leave their mark on the world.

The people who will be remembered are those philanthropic multi-millionaire entrepreneurs attempting to eradicate curable diseases and help those less well off in the world. These people understand their duty in the world: that they will never, could never, spend all the money they have, and that it can make a real life-changing difference to others.

Scottish/American entrepreneur Andrew Carnegie set the standard by giving to a variety of educational initiatives, and did much to kick-start philanthropic capitalism (despite being something of a bastard to do business with). Today we have Bill Gates (and many others) who may be just as hard to do business with, but who also do incredible work in efforts to cure malaria and Aids, alongside wealthy buddy Warren Buffett.

This is what the legacy of an entrepreneur and business leader should be all about. In a world of interfering and often hopeless (and self-serving) governments, it is only the entrepreneurial spirit that will work towards overcoming these sorts of problems.

This is not an exhaustive list of how to avoid failure, but it is a start. Beware greed, do not lose focus, concentrate on the detail and really understand your business, are just some of the vital lessons to learn. And do not upset Vladimir Putin, of course.

The world is full of people having great ideas. They are in coffee shops, around dinner tables, in school common rooms and in the bath. 'This time next year,' exclaimed Del Boy Trotter in UK comedy show *Only Fools and Horses*, 'we'll be millionaires!' But ideas are the easy bit. It is one thing to come up with an idea; another thing entirely to implement that idea, get the business up and running and operate it successfully. There are no guarantees of even short-term success, and the odds are against it. The law of nature is all about the survival of the fittest, and there is no doubt that some of the entrepreneurs in this book have survived against the odds. But nature takes its course.

That is not to say it is not worth bothering to try. Many millions of entrepreneurs around the world provide jobs and employment, create wealth, and drive society forward. It is certainly worth trying, and even failing is better than not trying at all.

There is no doubt that most of the people in this book have done incredibly well, but they have also got it badly wrong. They went too far, paid little attention to their businesses, starting believing their own hype, took their eyes off the ball or simply turned crooked.

While there are many failures out there, companies such as Microsoft, IBM, American Express, Tesco, Marks & Spencer and Google have defied the odds and show that it really is possible to achieve a dream.

It is great that all of those featured in this book had the guts and wherewithal to start and grow a business in the first place. They all took chances, built great things, and provided jobs and created wealth for others. They pursued an opportunity and made the most of it, and they should rightly be praised for that. If there is one lesson to take from this book, it is the belief in risk-responsible entrepreneurialism.

But many here sowed the seeds for their own demise. Others, of course, had it coming.

Jacob Rothschild, when asked about the consistent and enduring success of the Rothschild entrepreneurial dynasty, reportedly replied, 'I am not sure that we are all that successful. After all we always seem to sell too early and sell too cheap.'

Take heed – and try not to blow it.

Index